Evaluation Without Fear

Roger Kaufman
Susan Thomas

NEW VIEWPOINTS

A Division of Franklin Watts/New York/London

Acknowledgment

Special thanks are due to Bernadine and Robert Stake for their contributions in terms of materials to cite and review, to Howard Stoker for references and materials which would not have otherwise been included, and to Robert Stakenas for suggestions on the sections on needs assessment and its relation to evaluation.

NEW VIEWPOINTS
A Division of Franklin Watts
730 Fifth Avenue
New York, New York 10019

Library of Congress Cataloging in Publication Data

Kaufman, Roger
Evaluation Without Fear

Bibliography: p.
  Includes index.
    1. Organizational effectiveness.
2. Organization—Evaluation.   I. Thomas,
Susan, joint author.   II. Title.
HD58.9.K38   658.4′013   80-314
ISBN 0-531-06371-2
ISBN 0-531-06502-2 pbk.

CONTENTS

INTRODUCTION

When you evaluate, you want to see what has occurred in any activity or institution, how the results match your original intent, and whether or not what you did was really worth doing. The results could be useful, neutral, or unworthy. Evaluation will tell you that and will help you work toward constructive change or toward maintaining what is working well.

Evaluation covers almost the whole span of activity in an organization. Whether you are working in a mental health center, a counseling office, a school district, a health care unit, or even in a business office, evaluation still has the same rationale and the same basic components.

Evaluation deals with results, intended and unintended. The questions asked during evaluation are usually the same. Regardless of the context, evaluation seeks to answer the following questions:

1. What are the goals and objectives of the organization?
2. What should be the goals and objectives of the organization?

3. What results were intended by the program, project, activity, or organization?
4. What results were obtained by the program, project, activity, or organization?
5. What were the value and usefulness of the methods and means used to achieve the results?
6. How well was the program, project, activity, or organization administered and managed?
7. What, if anything, about the program, project, activity, or organization should be changed?
8. What, if anything, about the program, project, activity, or organization should be continued?
9. Should the organization, project, program, or activity exist at all?

These questions are basic. They probe the issue of activities and the worth of these activities in terms of what they accomplished.

Evaluation is more than testing or measuring; it includes asking and answering basic questions about efforts and results.

Evaluation is becoming more important for virtually everyone in education, training, and program development in institutions ranging from schools to industry to hospitals. This is the result of a societal trend that won't go away, namely, the growing demand from the public and from agencies in all areas for public program accountability—for a clearer measurement of the value of or return on the programs that hard-earned and inflation-burned money is going into. Just about everything in our economic and political life points to even more stringent demands along those lines, and evaluation is critical in giving us answers— telling us what value we get for what we put into things. What did we give and what did we get?

It's no accident that more leaders of existing programs or those seeking funds for new programs find themselves under pressure for new, better, more precise or more meaningful evaluations. And many programs where evaluation was, often rightly, seen as a ritual one had to perform to get money—a ritual that was not taken too seriously—are now finding themselves out on a limb, cut off, or in serious trouble.

This book is about evaluation and valuation. It is designed to tell you, as a person trained in your professional area and probably not an expert in evaluation, how to ask and answer basic questions about evaluation and valuation. We do not expect you to be an expert in evaluation. We do expect you to be a caring, competent person who wants to find answers that will make you and your organization more effective, efficient, and successful.

The book is written for a general audience. The authors have worked in a variety of areas—mental and physical health care, education, business, industry, and the military. We have noticed that while the content might vary (from nursing techniques to teaching techniques), almost all professionals are interested in interventions and positive change.

While reading this book, you will note that we use examples from a variety of disciplines. We do this to let you know that the techniques and tools are the same for all human activities and to encourage you to apply these understandings to your organization and your evaluation efforts.

Roger Kaufman
Susan Thomas
Tallahassee, Florida
April 1980

1

THE SCOPE AND NATURE OF EVALUATION

Evaluation may determine what is working, what is not working, what to change, and what to keep. Evaluation is a process used to assess the quality of what is going on.

Evaluators have often been confused with judges and auditors. The term *evaluation* often conjures up threat and blame-placing. This is an incorrect use and interpretation of evaluation.

Evaluation, if used correctly, will provide quality control by determining the gaps between what happened and what should have happened. The data coming from an evaluation should be used only to determine changes in organizational efforts and results—never to place blame.

In the fields of education, health or social service, we are interested in the quality and usefulness of that which we do and accomplish. Evaluation is the process by which we can assure that. Evaluation will tell us what is useful, what is not, and how to improve what requires improvement.

In evaluation, we can see results (data) as providing two kinds of evidence. One type of evidence is circumstantial, the other prima facie. From circumstantial evidence we can infer that something happened. For instance, there were low comprehension scores on the citizenship test; therefore, citizenship performance will be poor.

From a statement of this nature, we infer that there is a relationship, but we cannot be certain of the linkage. In law we might see a smoking gun and a dead body, and the circumstances indicate that the two are related. Much of what we do in education or training is based on circumstantial evidence.

We can have more confidence in prima facie evidence—evidence that is verifiable. We might not only see the smoking gun and the dead body, but have several witnesses who observed that the man in question did pull the trigger.

In public service we want to better establish prima facie evidence. One way to accomplish this is to trace our activities and results and relate them to organizational efforts and results, and finally to social impacts.

Finally, the purpose of evaluation is to collect data (results), convert the data into information (that which aids in making a useful decision), and use the information to make decisions. If decisions are not made, the evaluation might just as well have been skipped.

Unlike some others who have defined evaluation, we strongly urge that the process include the decision to change, modify, or keep that which is going on. The decision and the results of the decision are very much a part of useful evaluation. Evaluation has purpose, and it has results. It has to have impact.

WORDS AND MEANINGS— WHERE EVALUATION FITS

Evaluation is an area which has been experiencing growth, development, and change. It used to be primarily concerned with determining the relationships between intentions and performance, but recently its horizons have been broadening. With these changes in the field, there have been some changes in the definitions of words and terms, and frankly, there is much confusion today.

In this section we will define our terms, perhaps not always in the same way as other authors do, but in a manner that will let us be consistent and precise throughout this book. The words and related concepts we now cover are:

Goals
Objectives
Needs assessment and needs
Planning
Evaluating
Testing
Measurement
Results
Means and ends

GOALS

Anytime we have a statement of purpose, we have a goal. There are a number of kinds of goals, but they all state, usually by naming or relating, *where we want to be*. Examples might be to: improve reading; achieve good self-concept; get to Boston; build an ambulatory health care unit in Mesa; increase the number of graduates; decrease the number of dropouts; improve mental health; reduce the incidence of disease.

Goals may be set for an organization, a society, or a job. (See Chapter 4.) Sometimes we find it useful to be quite precise in expressing our intended purposes; we want to have more rigor than would be achieved by just stating our intentions in terms of a label or a relationship and these statements are called objectives.

OBJECTIVES

While goals state intentions in general terms of naming or comparing, objectives are more precise. Goals simply say that some *thing* (nursing care, reading scores) should be better or higher than before, but don't say by how *much*. Objectives state *exactly* where we are going and how we know when we have arrived. Objectives are precise statements of intended accomplishments.

An objective has four characteristics, and it is a statement which tells:

1. What results are to be achieved.
2. Who or what will demonstrate these results.
3. The conditions under which we will observe the extent to which the results have been achieved.
4. The specific criteria to be used to determine achievement.

All of these elements are stated in such a way that there will be no confusion among workers as to what is intended.

Both goals and objectives are used to determine where one is going, and once stated, help us compare the intentions with the results. Objectives should be used wherever possible. They are more precise and thus allow for more rigorous and successful planning and evaluation.

NEEDS AND NEEDS ASSESSMENT

Objectives (and goals) tell us about what we want to achieve. They give a statement of intended results.

But what do we do when:

- we are not sure what it is we *should be* achieving?
- we know there are some goals and objectives, but we want to make sure that they are complete?
- we know what our organization is now accomplishing, and what it aimed to accomplish but want to know what we should be accomplishing?

Needs assessment is used when we want to find out, document, and state clearly *what should be* in terms of results, and relate that to the results now being achieved.

A need is a measurable gap between *what is* and *what should be*. By a systematic process, we may determine the gaps between what is and what should be, place those gaps in priority order, and select the ones of highest priority for action. This systematic method of comparing what is with what should be, including the determination of what should be, is the hallmark of needs assessment. It is a creative act from which we may derive goals and objectives not previously identified and accepted.

PLANNING

We plan when we want to achieve something. If we want to get from where we are to where we know we want to be (achieve an existing set of objectives), then we can plan that trip. When we want to identify heretofore nonexistent goals and objectives, a more fundamental variety of planning is required.

For now, let's say only that when goals and objectives are existing and acceptable, we use one variety of planning. (We will call this *internal* planning in order to show that we are working within an organization and are accepting its goals and objectives.) However, when we want to consider the possibility of creating new goals and objectives, or verifying the correctness of existing ones, another variety of planning is required. (We will call this creative planning model *external* planning in order to show that it takes the frame of reference outside of the organization and into society.) So there are two major varieties of planning: internal and external. One allows for the creation or addition of new goals and objectives; the other does not. Planning in both involves the accomplishment of purposes in a systematic manner.

EVALUATION AND NEEDS ASSESSMENT

Evaluation is a process of helping to make things better than they are, of improving the situation. Evaluation can help you answer these questions: Did my actions make a difference? Was it worth my effort? What should be changed to reach the objectives? Evaluation allows us to identify and document any gaps between our current results and our desired results. Evaluation tells us how we are doing compared with what we set out to do, and will suggest, by the gaps identified and documented, what might be done to achieve our objectives.

Sometimes evaluation is confused with needs assessment or the two terms are used interchangeably. A needs assessment will show us what it is we should be doing in the first place, while an evaluation will tell us how well we are doing in an ongoing operation. There are a number of types of needs assessment that address various kinds of gaps in any system. We will take a closer look at the types of needs assessment in Chapter 3. For now, you should just be aware that evaluation and needs assessment are not the same thing, but that both are very important.

EVALUATION, TESTING, AND MEASUREMENT

Sometimes these terms are used interchangeably. What do they really mean? Are they the same things?

They are not the same thing. There really is a difference among testing, measurement, and evaluation. Briefly, *testing* is the task of gathering data, *measurement* the technique or method used to compare those data against a standard, and *evaluation* the purpose for which one uses tests and measurements. Now, let's look at each term more closely.

TESTING

Testing is the piece of work to be done, the gathering of information to be used in evaluation. It is the process of administering an instrument, such as a standardized test of some sort, to gather data.

We have to select the appropriate test, the one that will best measure the skills, knowledge, and attitudes of the individuals and groups being studied and evaluated. We have to make decisions about whether to use norm-referenced tests (where each person's performance is compared with that of all others taking the test), or criterion-referenced tests (where each person's performance is compared with a known standard). Without the appropriate test and the correct resulting data, how good will our evaluation be? (The Appendix gives more detailed information about testing.)

Related to the testing process is measurement, or that particular technique we use to compare data. Let's look at what measurement is all about.

MEASUREMENT

Measurement is the process whereby the data collected are compared with a standard. It includes the tools and techniques used in the testing process, but goes beyond that. We give a test to collect performance data. When we compare the performance with existing criteria, we are measuring the degree or extent of something. Thus, if we are interested in controlling hypertension in a sample of males, we can arrange to take their blood pressure and other samples; we can test their hypertension by using instruments. When we actually record the data and compare the actual with the standard, we are measuring. So, when we put the cuff around a patient's arm and pump it up in order to get a pressure reading, we are testing. When we read the data and compare it, we are measuring. The test, then, is the tool used to get the data; comparing the data to a standard is measurement.

There are four different types of yardsticks used in measurement. Each type has different characteristics and is useful in different situations. The four types or scales of measurement are: *nominal, ordinal, interval*, and *ratio*. These four yardsticks give different types of information. We must be able to specify the type of information we require, and then select our tool accordingly.

NOMINAL DATA

One scale of measurement commonly used by all of us is *naming*. People have names (Charles, Jack, Shirley, Susan), and we note that they are different. There are no implications that one is better than another; they are just different. This type of measuring scale is called *nominal*. In the case of nominal data, we are simply using numbers as labels. The numbers in and of themselves have no meaning and are arbitrary designations for different categories.

If we are interested in nominal level data, which means being able to group things and count them, we could observe the number of different kinds of events that occur, for example, how many cars of each make were sold during the month of June. We could have categories for Chevrolet, Ford, Pontiac, and others. If we wished, we could substitute a number for the name, but this would be arbitrary. The numbers would have no special meaning; they would just be labels. Another example of nominal data is a series of questions that can be answered yes or no and that do not reflect any kind of ranking or ordering of information. Do you have blond hair? Did you learn something today? We can put such responses into categories, but we can't do much more. There is no means of determining that "not blond" is better than "blond," or vice versa. The answers are simply categories, and if we assigned numbers to these categories, the numbers would be labels and nothing more. It is usually pretty difficult to identify and quantify gaps with nominal data—just naming and labeling.

ORDINAL DATA

Another scale of measurement that is more reliable (consistent and repeatable) is one in which we note that something is greater than, less than, or equal to other things. It is the "beauty contest scale" in that we rank things as more or less beautiful, useful, or attractive. This ranking scale is called *ordinal*. It does not tell how much more or less two things of adjacent ranks are. It just tells that they are equal, less than, or more than each other.

This second yardstick, or ordinal scale, also can provide information through simple observation. If we wanted to determine which person is tallest, we can line up a group of people according to height and assign the shortest person a rank of 1, the next a rank of 2, and so on. The assigned numbers would designate the order in terms of height, but without measuring we would not know how much taller the person of rank 3 is than the person of rank 1.

Being able to rank people or data does provide us with some information, but only about the order. We learn nothing about how far the ranks are apart. So, for gathering precise, reliable information about needs and gaps, a "better" scale would be more useful.

MOST USEFUL, THE INTERVAL SCALE

The third, or *interval scale*, can indicate not only that something is more or less than something else, but also how far apart they are on some dimension. For example, we might note that the temperature outside is 77 degrees Fahrenheit, that the high for the day was 83 degrees, and that the difference between the two temperatures is 6 degrees. Each degree on the Fahrenheit scale is equal to every other degree. The only thing arbitrary is the starting point. We arbitrarily agree on what zero degrees means. In this case, it means we simply all agree to start counting from that zero point and note that there are equal scale differences. It is important to remember that on the interval scale, a zero does not mean an absence of something.

Most measurement in psychology, education, and human behavior is in this form, giving us many tools and techniques from which to choose. For example, most of the achievement tests we use are considered to be interval measurement. Likewise, many of the attitude scales, interest inventories, and aptitude batteries are examples of interval measurements. Some people even consider IQ tests to be a form of interval measurement.

This type of measurement is more reliable than either nominal or ordinal scales of measurement. We can do many things statistically with this type of data. In the process of needs assessment, we can determine what level of achievement a child should have (the standard of comparison)—for example, a score of 50 on an achievement test. Then we can administer the test and determine the discrepancy between what is and what should be. We can also go about selecting some alternatives to lessen the identified gap, with more confidence in the precise "amount" of the gap, and being better able to recognize when we have closed it.

THE RATIO SCALE

Finally, there is the most reliable scale of all: *ratio*. Here we have equal scale distances and a known, fixed, and meaningful zero point. We know what zero feet is, and we know exactly how much one foot is, five feet, and fifty feet. These are ratio scale measures, and they are quite reliable and quite precise. Unfortunately, there are not many useful things in human behavior that merit measurement on a ratio scale. Because of the requirement of an absolute and meaningful zero or beginning point, many of the ratio scales have to do with physical measurements: weight, length, and volume. Something like typing ability, measured in words correctly typed per minute, is an example of a ratio scale. But how often can you use a scale such as this?

APPLYING SCALES OF MEASUREMENT

Usually, the best alternative is the interval level of measurement. You can do most things with it, it is fairly reliable, and it can be quite useful in quantifying gaps. And, it is a useful thing to be able to say exactly how wide a particular gap is.

Let's try to identify some measurement tools and determine what kind of data they provide.

Tool	*Kind of Data*
Counting the number of sit-ups completed	
Observing alertness in children and ranking all children in the class	
Administering a mathematics achievement test	
Asking children whether or not they ate breakfast	

Did you identify the first tool as yielding ratio data? It's possible that someone completed no sit-ups, so there would be a meaningful zero or starting point. Observing the alertness in children and then ranking the children would provide ordinal data. Giving the mathematics achievement test would probably provide you with interval data. Asking the children whether they ate breakfast would give you nominal data: the number of children who ate breakfast and the number who did not.

In review, then, things that can be observed, including many kinds of behaviors, are usually at the nominal or ordinal level of measurement. Even if you use some of the observation schedules that have been carefully designed and developed, the resulting data will, in most cases, be at the nominal or ordinal level. When things may be compared in terms of how much they relate, or to the degree of differences or similarities there are between them, then we use interval or ratio scales of measurement. The more we can have confidence in the differences that we measure, and the precision with which we may say how far apart they are, the more reliable the measurement. In an evaluation, we attempt to meaningfully measure using an interval (and occasionally a ratio) scale of measurement. But only when it makes sense to do so. Precision for its own sake is not worthwhile. Neat perhaps, but not worthy.

GOALS AND OBJECTIVES REVISITED

Now we may make a distinction between goals and objectives using what we now know about scales of measurement: Goals are statements of results which are measurable on a nominal or ordinal scale of measurement, and an objective is measurable on an interval or ratio scale. The difference between goals and objectives is one of precision and reliability, not one of purpose or direction. Goals may be converted into objectives by making them more "measurable"—more precise, so that they are measurable on an interval or ratio scale. Sometimes, however, we cannot usefully measure something on an interval or ratio scale, so we settle, considering the current state of knowledge, for goals.

THE GOALS OF EVALUATION

Testing, measurement, and evaluation—those are terms which are often bothersome. They often conjure up feelings of personal inadequacy and an inability to deal with numbers. There are also concerns, often justified, that evaluation means censure. The terms *evaluation*, *testing*, and *measurement* sound depersonalizing, and some educators infer that people are being separated from their humanity, competence, caring, and sensitivity.

Good evaluation does not confuse those concepts with blaming and buck-passing. The evaluation you will learn in this book uses testing (data collecting), measurement (the method of applying standards to behaviors), and evaluation to place values and worth among alternative activities, events, and results. It is sensitive to that which is difficult and tricky to measure and decide, and it takes into account the human characteristics that often get lost in other evaluation efforts. Good evaluation is humane and humanistic.

Many evaluation books and efforts relate only to goals, objectives, planning, testing, and measurement. They determine only the extent and worth of *what is*.

We are trying to add another dimension to your understanding and competence—the possibility of relating evaluation to useful change—what should be.

In the material which follows, we are going to make a number of distinctions which are different from much of what is currently being used in the field of evaluation. We want evaluation to be more than a reactive statement comparing that which has been accomplished with that which was intended; and move to consideration of the new, the useful, the creative in terms of possible purposes and needs.

RESULTS

Why should we be concerned about results? Because results are what we are charged with accomplishing. If we are teachers, we are asked to bring about valued and valuable learning. If we are nurses, we are expected to bring people back to health; if we are counselors, we are responsible for helping people to help themselves to become happy and productive. Actually, all people, in some way or another, are usually responsible as agents for bringing about change. Education is designed to help people become self-sufficient and contribute, and other helping professions are designed to help others help themselves to achieve self-sufficiency and contribute. All find it productive and creative to increase happiness and self-satisfaction along the way. Thus, all of us are *intervention specialists*. We are responsible for intervening between people and their environment to get results such as competence in reading or writing, health maintenance to allow for occupational and personal activity, mental well-being to be happy and productive.

Looked at in another way, we attempt to close gaps between current results—such as poor mental or physical health, inability to read and write, inability to get and keep a job—and desired results—earning respect, getting along with family and community, earning more than one spends, staying physically fit.

Gaps are discrepancies between current results and desired results. The more precisely and consistently we are able to measure the gaps, the higher the probability of our being able to: 1) determine what should be done to close them, and 2) assure that we can pick the best means to achieve the desired results.

Just about everything in the use of evaluation is concerned with gaps. This makes our understanding of evaluation easier, for it lets us simplify the world (sometimes a little artificially) into looking at gaps between what is and what should be. It also helps us to sort our world into "bundles" that are easier to understand and handle—easier than what William James once described as a "blooming, buzzing mess."

There are different kinds of gaps. Some of our concern will be for gaps in means, and some will be for gaps in results. Let's look at that more closely.

MEANS AND ENDS

Means are the ways we choose to get things done (such as a curriculum, education, nursing, using automobiles, writing) and *ends* are the results of one or more means (such as surviving in the world, being able to diagnose your own symptoms of illness, being able to read well enough to apply for a job, being able to get and keep a job, being able to maintain health well enough to stay out of a hospital).

Means and ends are often confused in our world, but they can provide us with powerful understanding. We use means to achieve ends. Means are tools and techniques; ends are the results we want.

Check each item as to whether it is a means or an end:

	MEANS	END
Knitting		
Fever thermometer		
Reading course		
Job entry skills		
Money		
Courses		
Graduation		
Self-sufficiency		

Here is the way we see them:

	MEANS	END
Knitting	X	
Fever thermometer	X	
Reading course	X	

	MEANS	END
Job entry skills		X
Money	X	
Courses	X	
Graduation		X
Self-sufficiency		X

Actually, the most basic end listed above is self-suffi-ciency. It is the most important thing to anyone, for without physical survival, nothing else makes much difference. Money is not a useful end in and of itself. You cannot eat or drink it; you can only use it to obtain goods and services from others; therefore, it's a means.

Evaluation can be related to the means of an "interven-tion" or to the ends, or results of the intervention. For instance, we could measure the gap between current reading skills, knowledges, and attitudes, and that which is necessary to get and keep a job. Means and ends. Both are important and both are the rightful subject of evaluation.

APPLYING THE CONCEPTS

Let's look at an example of how it might work—how all of these concepts might fit together in a typical applica-tion, using this hypothetical example:

A nurse, in her fifth year at the regional medical center, suggested that a new burn center was required. She talked it over with the assistant director of nursing, then—together with the director of nursing—spoke with the medical director, who gave her approval to pursue it further. The director liked the idea so much that a two thousand dollar budget was put at her disposal.

She realized that the burn center was a means—a possible way to measurably improve the health and well-being of people in the region. She also realized that it might not be the most important means for improving physical health and well-being, so she thought that she should determine, exactly, what the needs of the community were. Thus, she could relate means and ends, and see if the burn center was really the most useful means for the regional medical center. Getting the needs assessment under way was a bit difficult, for she had to determine "what is" and "what should be" for the region. In order to do that she had to measure its current physical health status, and compare it with acceptable standards, and determine the gaps between the current results and desired results. Measurement was required to compare the two poles of "what is" and "what should be."

She had to collect data, and she identified some previous research efforts in which useful survey forms for collecting the data had been developed. She decided to use these instruments to collect the necessary data, for they fit her situation and problems very well in that they collected data on results. She was then able to measure the differences between "what is" and "what should be." The measurements were based upon the data collected (testing).

In order to determine "what should be" she had to determine performance standards. She obtained these from national health studies which defined the minimal requirements for physical health. Thus, these criteria served as the reference standards required for measurement.

Based upon this determination of gaps between current physical health levels and required ones, she could set goals for physical health in the region. She then was able to find out how much of the deviation from that standard accounted for the main causes of poor physical health, including nutrition, heart disease, accidents, poisoning, and so on. She found that burns were only a small (but very important) part of the health-care needs, and that the region was really more deficient in coronary care.

Using these data and the resulting measurements and needs, she recommended that a coronary care unit be set up, listing goals as well as very precise objectives for what a successful coronary care unit would accomplish. She got a go-ahead to develop a plan for meeting those objectives. Her plan organized and sequenced all of the en-route results, ingredients, building resources, and how-to-do-its required to meet the objectives. And all of this was based upon an identification of needs—the gaps between current physical health in the region and required levels.

A few years later, after receiving state and government grants, a coronary care unit was approved, and the plans implemented. While the unit was being developed and put into operation, she (having been promoted to supervisor of this project) determined the gaps between the planned results and those being achieved and decided about what should be changed, and what should be continued. This en-route result (later on we will discuss this procedure), called a "formative evaluation," allowed her to decide what was working and what was not, and to better ensure that the goals and objectives for the center would be met.

And finally, after the first year of operation, she evaluated the sum of the total project by comparing the intended goals and objectives for coronary health with that which was achieved, and reported on the successes and shortfalls she found. (This end-of-project evaluation is called a "summative evaluation," and will also be described later.)

The needs assessment showed that building a burn center was secondary when something else was more critical to the region. From these data, another alternative means was identified, and goals and objectives for it derived. To do the needs assessment and goal setting, she used a form of testing (data collecting) and then compared the data with standards (measurement). After setting useful goals and objectives (they were based upon justified needs), she planned and evaluated the effort as it was being developed (formative evaluation); and after the first year of operation, to see if the results intended were being achieved (summative evaluation).

Goals, objectives, needs assessment, evaluation, planning, testing, and measurement are all useful tools for the professional who wants to achieve worthwhile results—on purpose.

KEY POINTS

- *Goals* state where we want to go; usually stated in nominal or ordinal scale terms, they point the direction to desired results. *Objectives* are more specific and precise statements of desired results that are stated in interval or ratio scale terms.
- *Needs assessment* is useful for determining if our goals or objectives are appropriate by determining the gaps between current results and those results we should be attempting to achieve. *Evaluation*, on the other hand, also looks at gaps in results, but only deals with those which are currently known. Needs assessment deals with gaps between "what is" and "what should be" and evaluation focuses upon gaps between "what is" and "what was intended." Needs assessment is usually seen when we are thinking of a new activity or project— before our developing and using interventions—and evaluation is seen during and after organizational efforts.
- *Planning* is a process by which we try to structure our methods and interventions in order to manage and orchestrate them to better ensure that we achieve our objectives and meet the needs we have identified.

- *Testing* is the process of collecting data, and *measurement* is taking that data and making some sense out of it by comparing that which was observed with some reference standard. Testing is usually useful for making measurements. Measurement is the method of comparing collected data against a standard. Methods may include, among other things, observations, questionnaires, and achievement tests. The data resulting from tests are compared against one of four standards: nominal, ordinal, interval, or ratio:
- *Nominal* measures only that something is different from something else by giving it a name or arbitrary label.
- *Ordinal* notes that two or more things are equal to, greater than, or less than each other.
- *Interval* notes how far apart two or more things are on a given dimension using equal appearing units.
- *Ratio* tells exactly how far apart two or more things are from each other and also how far they all are from a known and nonarbitrary starting point.

Selected References

1. Worthen, B. R., and Sanders, J. R. *Educational Evaluation: Theory and Practice.* Worthington, Ohio: C. A. Jones, 1973.
2. Popham, W. J. *Educational Evaluation.* Englewood Cliffs, N.J.: Prentice-Hall, 1975.
3. Hemphill, J. K. "The Relationship between Research and Evaluation Studies" in *Educational Evaluation: New Roles, New Means*, edited by R. W. Tyler. 68th Yearbook, National Society for the Study of Education, Part II. Chicago: NSSE, 1969.

4. Lewin, K. "Group Decision and Social Change" in *Readings in Social Psychology*, edited by Newcomb and Harley. New York: Harper, 1948.
5. Weber, E. *Early Childhood Education: Perspectives on Change*. Worthington, Ohio: C. A. Jones, 1970.
6. Gibbons, J. *Nonparametric Methods for Quantitative Analysis*. New York: Holt, Rinehart & Winston, 1976.
7. Kerlinger, F. N. *Foundations of Behavioral Research*. 2nd ed. New York: Holt, Rinehart & Winston, 1973.
8. Williamson, J. B., Karp, D. A., and Dalphin, J. R. *The Research Craft*. Boston: Little, Brown, 1977.
9. Bloom, B. S. "Some Theoretical Issues Relating to Educational Evaluation" in *Educational Evaluation: New Roles, New Means,* edited by R. W. Tyler. 68th Yearbook, National Society for the Study of Education, Part II. Chicago: NSSE, 1969.
10. Salasin, S. "An Interview with M. Scriven." *Evaluation* 1975, 2(1).
11. Kaufman, R. *Educational System Planning*. Englewood Cliffs, N.J.: Prentice-Hall, 1972.
12. Kaufman, R. *Identifying and Solving Problems: A System Approach*. 2nd ed. La Jolla, Calif.: University Associates Publishers, 1979.
13. Kaufman, R., and English, F. W. *Needs Assessment: Concept and Application*. Englewood Cliffs, N.J.: Educational Technology Publications, 1979.

2
THE CONTEXT FOR
THE EVALUATION
PROCESS

Evaluation helps us make sense out of our programs. It helps us see what works, what doesn't work, and why. We can keep the good parts, revise or discard the bad. Evaluation can be used for pieces or stages of any program or for the whole thing.

In this chapter, we will take a close look at the total process and its parts, defining the goals and objectives of organizations that provide the framework and rationale for any evaluation. Notice in particular our emphasis (this is where ours differs from most discussions of evaluation) on the final results and ultimate goals of the process. We present two hypothetical stories—one extended, one brief—in human terms; this is the process as seen by learners and professionals. Our scenarios are told in ways deliberately designed to emphasize the human and humane dimensions of evaluation. After setting the stage we will go into the different modes, strategies, and techniques of evaluation.

The following story is fictional. It is about a young woman—and a pretty sophisticated one at that (a liberty the authors can take)—and her progress and relationships.

While this example is taken from the world of education, the concepts behind it apply to other kinds of interventions: vocational training, occupational development, nursing, counseling, law, medicine, dentistry, just about any situation in which planned change is to occur, and in which we want to know what we have accomplished, what we intended to accomplish, and what we should have attempted to accomplish.

As you read this section, keep in mind that while the example is from education, the framework is general. After we are finished talking about Becky and relating her story to an *organizational elements model*, we will take you on another adventure, not with Becky, but with her mother as she deals with her status as a displaced homemaker.

In this story, we are showing the elements of education in relation to an actual learner. From this base, we are going to define five basic organizational elements and show you how they relate to each other and to the overall job of education (or any other intervention), and to the society in which organizational efforts and results are nested.

These elements will be the basis of this book, for evaluation should occur at each one. Additionally, evaluation should tell us not only how well each one worked, but how all of the elements worked together.

Let's now turn to Becky's first day at school and then follow her through her education.

THE PURPOSES OF EDUCATION

It is Monday, September 11, and Becky is going to school, starting her journey through learning and growing at Parker Elementary School. It is the first day, and her mother is driving her to school. Becky is excited and apprehensive: "What will it be like, really, mom? Will there be people there like me? Will I get along well with the other children? Will I learn to read? Why do I have to go to school?"

Becky was bubbling with questions, and they came much faster than her mother could answer. "Will I learn to print? Do we get to play? What happens if I don't learn?"

GETTING READY FOR LIFE

"Wait a minute, Becky," said her mother. "Let me answer your questions. School is a way in which we help you and other children to learn about our world and get ready to make the world a better place in which to live."

"I know, mom, but what is it all really like?"

"We should know why we do something, Becky. Then we can determine how to get it done. Remember when you wanted a new doll—right away? Remember that we talked and found that it was not the new doll that you wanted? You thought that Raggedy Ann was broken. Remember how we fixed Annie and that took away the necessity to get a new doll?"

"Yes, but . . ."

"Explaining education is pretty much the same. Before we begin some action, we should understand what it is we want to accomplish."

"Okay, mom," said Becky, hoping that this was not going to be a long lecture.

"As I said, we want children to know about the world so that they can help themselves and others to live better."

"So?" said Becky.

"So," said her mother, "schools are places where little girls like you and bigger children such as George can learn what is important in order to live in the world and make it better."

LEARNING USEFUL TOOLS

"I thought we learned how to read and write."

"Sure, we learn ways to cope with our world, such as reading, writing, and figuring—a lot of things, Becky, which will help us as we go through school. When you graduate, what you learned will help you take your place as a person who works, as a mother, or perhaps both."

"Mom, I don't understand. I thought we went to school to learn how to read and write. You're talking about things that are far away—working and being a mother and stuff like that."

"Thanks for telling me how well I made myself clear, Becky. Let me try again."

MEANS AND ENDS

Her mother thought for a moment. She wanted to get across to Becky that there was a difference but also a relationship between means and ends. Education, she thought, is a means to helping people achieve the ends: self-sufficiency and the ability to contribute. Means and ends, she thought, how can I explain them to Becky?

"Becky, there is a difference between the tools we use to fix something and getting that something fixed."

"Huh?"

"Remember how you learned to use a needle and thread to patch up Annie?"

"Yes."

"Well, the tools were the needle and thread, and the result was that you now enjoy a good-as-new Raggedy Ann."

"Okay, so?"

"In school, you have the opportunity to learn about and use the tools you'll use when you get out of school—reading and writing, the use of numbers, getting along with and understanding others, learning how to bring yourself understanding and pleasure, all of the tools to help you and others be self-sufficient and to contribute later on."

ACHIEVING DIFFERENCES

"Mom, let me see if I understand. School is getting me ready to be an adult like you and daddy. I have to learn all of the things you learned so I can be just like you. Right?"

"Almost, Becky," said her mother. "We don't want you to be just like anybody but yourself. You can learn from dad and me and George and from just about everyone in the world, including your teachers, but you are going to learn to think and to reason, how to be healthy and how to be happy with yourself, and how to grow and continue to be the unique, special person that you are. We don't want everyone to be the same, although a lot of us might think the same way about certain things, such as how to keep the environment clean and how we shouldn't kill one another."

"So I go to school to help me be a good adult, right, mom?"

"Right."

Mom hoped that she had gotten the main point across to Becky—that school is not an end in itself but is a means to help Becky grow and develop so that she could become a happy, contributing adult.

EDUCATION AS A MEANS

Education is a process, just as Becky's mother explained to her. It gives us a set of tools and techniques that our society uses to help children grow, develop, and contribute.

Education provides tools, techniques, and procedures that have been selected to help children learn, develop, and become increasingly able to live productive, independent lives. Education is a means; the ends are people who are self-sufficient and who contribute in our world. They are not dependent upon others for handouts or charity.

SKILLS, KNOWLEDGE, AND ATTITUDES

The objective of education is to foster the development of useful skills, knowledge, and attitudes in learners. This results in changes in behavior. If education did not intend to change behavior, it could simply become a baby-sitting service.

CHANGING . . .

The difficult aspect of this intention to change behavior is determining what behavior to change and then making sure not only that changes happen but also that they are useful changes.

. . . ON PURPOSE

Education, then, is "done on purpose." It is not a "happening" where teachers and learners come together and let the chips fall where they may. The responsibility for purposeful change is enormous.

If we are going to evaluate education, then we have to know what was intended and compare that with what actually did happen. Evaluation relates intended ends to actual ends and also frequently relates the means, or activities, to the accomplishments to determine the worth and efficiency of those activities.

THE ORGANIZATIONAL ELEMENTS APPLIED TO EDUCATION

Let's follow Becky into her school and observe what happens. By examining what she will be experiencing as she makes her learning journey through school, we will be able to identify some of the elements of education and define them. We will be building, step by step, a model of organizational efforts and results, and of societal impact. Ready?

GOALS AND PURPOSES

After driving Becky to school, checking in with the assistant principal and being assured that the preregistration was effective, Becky's mother took Becky to her assigned classroom. Mr. Llewelyn, the kindergarten teacher, explained the schedule and the room arrangement. He told them that he would be assisted by a teaching aide, parents, occasional visiting consultants in art and science, and a nurse. He told

Becky the goals for kindergarten: to get ready for reading and using numbers, to get in touch with her body, to see herself as unique and worthwhile, to learn to grow and observe, to learn about other people, to take their wishes and feelings into consideration, to stand up for her rights without interfering with the rights of others, and to take increasing responsibility for her own learning, growth, and behavior.

Becky was awed and a bit apprehensive. The teacher had used some words she did not understand.

Mr. Llewelyn took her to her seat and introduced her to Sam, Marie, Juan, and Beth, who sat near her. The other children were feeling a bit more comfortable than Becky, and they showed her around the classroom, pointing out the reading center, the flannel boards and the materials posted there, the pre-primers stacked on the shelf, the building blocks and puzzles—all of the materials she and the other children would be using to help them learn. Becky looked around, and her thoughts wandered. Just what would be happening to her in this unusual place?

THE RESOURCES AND "INGREDIENTS" OF EDUCATION—INPUTS

THE TOOLS AND RESOURCES

Becky was coming to grips with the "inputs" of the educational system: the tools and resources that are made available to help achieve the objectives of education.

They include: learners, teachers, teaching aides, consultants, schools, other buildings, administrators, desks, chairs, learning resources, money, the goals and objectives of education, in fact, all of the ingredients of education.

INPUTS

We refer to them as *inputs* because they represent that which we put into the system including goals and objectives we wish to accomplish. Inputs, then, are our basic resources. They include a statement of where we are going and what is available to get us there.

In the story of Becky's adventure into "educationland" we noted that Mr. Llewelyn told Becky and her mother about the goals he intended for himself, for the learners, and for the school system to accomplish ("to get ready for reading and using numbers, to get in touch with her body, to see herself as unique . . ."). He also told about other inputs including resource people, the physical layout, the schedule. The other children showed Becky some of the materials that were available to help facilitate learning. These materials are inputs also. Inputs are the resources that can be used, including the learners and the teachers. Together learners and educators seek and use the resources to achieve learning success.

We start with the inputs. Next we use those inputs (ingredients) to achieve our goals and objectives.

Let us observe Becky a bit longer.

USING THE RESOURCES AND TOOLS OF EDUCATION—PROCESSES

Becky did not have long to wonder about her new role and the educational process. After her mother left, Mr. Llewelyn walked to his desk and looked around his classroom. Everything was in order, and he was ready to start. The children seemed to know they should quiet down without being asked, and within thirty seconds their attention was riveted on the teacher. Formal education was about to begin for Becky.

SCHOOL CAN BE FUN

"Fun," said Mr. Llewelyn. "School is fun. It is going to be fun to be here and fun to learn."

The children looked at each other and most smiled.

"We are here to learn, to grow, to be happy," he continued. "We are going to work in groups at times and at other times as individuals. I want these children over here," he said, pointing to Becky, Juan, Sam, Marie, and Beth, along with three others, "to meet me in the reading circle, and I want the rest of you to play in the construction area. Those in the construction area are to build an apartment of the future."

Mr. Llewelyn was getting right into the swing of things. He was implementing the suggestions in the District Curriculum Guide and getting the children functioning in group activity areas. During the summer, he and other kindergarten and first grade teachers in the district had held a seminar to learn about team teaching and team building. They had written behavioral objectives and made lesson plans. The principal of each teacher's school had received and approved the plans and objectives.

USING A PLAN

Later in the summer, he and fifteen other teachers in the district had asked for and been invited to attend a special workshop on learning and child growth and development. The interest in that dual topic came up when Mr. Llewelyn and several others realized that tools and techniques to help improve learning were best understood when you know about the children, their growth and development, and how they learn. It had been a good review for him and for the other teachers, and he had a much better understanding of how and when to use the various teaching methods, tools, and materials that were available to him. He was ready to begin.

He walked to the reading area, noted that the children were sitting in a vague approximation of a circle and asked them to form a better circle. They did. He glanced at the construction area and noted that everyone was waiting quietly.

TOOLS AT WORK

"A good start," he thought to himself. Then he said aloud, "Boys and girls, we are going to start the fun. We are going to get ready to read using the Growth Reading materials that were developed and tested just for children such as you—to help you learn to relate pictures and words."

He had prepared to use the packaged materials, and now he started to present them with cards and asked each child to think of what was pictured on each card, to think of the name and be ready to tell the others what had been shown. He had been trained to use these learning materials last year and was convinced that they were good, and he had research data showing that the materials worked with children similar to those in the Parker School. His mind flashed to what he would do for the rest of the day and even the rest of the semester. He knew that the teachers had worked with an open school and that they were readying a building plan which would allow the halls and passageways in the elementary area to be open to learning activities. He was anxious and a bit apprehensive about keeping discipline in this new setup. He thought of the testing plan, which would be based upon what children actually knew and were able to do as well as the old, more familiar norm-referenced tests such as he and others had taken when they were in school. His mind raced now, not noticing that the children had been looking at his card for twenty seconds—more time than was required. Suddenly he focused his attention on the group once again and asked Becky to tell the class what the picture was.

"A cow," Becky said proudly, and the other children nodded.

"How about this one?" Llewelyn asked, shifting to a new card. His mind leaped ahead again as he thought about the new counseling program, which would have children interact with others, and about learning options in the world of work and about jobs they could hold when they grew up.

He thought of the new girls' football team to be tried for the first time, and he thought of the noncompetitive athletics program to be initiated this fall.

SENSIBLE INNOVATION

"This school is really progressive," he thought to himself. "They are always trying new things to help kids learn."

This is the way he thought education should be, and Tom Llewelyn was proud and pleased to be just where he was.

METHODS AND TECHNIQUES

Becky and the rest of the class were experiencing the "process" of education. These are all of the ways and means that educators use to bring about learning and growth. The processes are the methods and techniques for using the resources and people of education—the ways of doing things.

PROCESS

Processes in education include such things as the way teachers teach and help learners (such as staffing patterns and instructional materials designed to help students learn); the way in which the physical plant is organized and used (such as the open-school plan in Becky's new school where the children were allowed to move freely from their homeroom to the library or other activity centers); the curriculum and curriculum guides (such as the one that Tom Llewelyn had developed with the other teachers in order to plan and deliver education in the coming year).

"DOING" EDUCATION

The processes of education are all of the how-to-do-its we use to achieve our desired results. The processes are the "doing" part of the system. If it is the manner in which education is delivered, if it includes the use of the tools and techniques of education, then it is a process. Our stewardship of education is most clearly observed during the process, for it is here that we see what it is that educators and children do when education is being delivered.

Most of our attention in education has traditionally been devoted to the processes of education. The process is best determined by the characteristics of the learners and what it is they should know and be able to do when they leave our schools. The processes are the means of education; the results are the ends.

EN-ROUTE RESULTS:
TEACHER & LEARNER
ACCOMPLISHMENTS—PRODUCTS

Becky is learning as she works in her classroom. Mr. Llewelyn has her demonstrate her learning in a series of tests or activities. These tests allow her to demonstrate what she knows to herself and to her teacher to make sure that she knows what she should know and that both she and the teacher know she has mastered the lesson.

As Becky goes through school there will be a number of such opportunities for her to demonstrate mastery. There will be tests to be taken, books to be finished, and classes to complete. As Becky is educated she will be learning and demonstrating what she has learned. Every class she completes will be a milestone in her educational progress. These are the en-route results. When she passes a test or completes elementary school and middle school, Becky will have completed an en-route activity, and these are called *products*. A product is any en-route accomplishment. It may also be a lesson that has worked, that has been validated and demonstrated as useful.

PRODUCTS

Products are numerous in education, and Becky will experience many before she exits from the school system.

There are many accomplishments that occur in one's school career that are called products: courses completed, tests passed, lessons mastered, instructional materials and procedures proven to meet their objectives—in short, any result which is along the route to where one is going. Most of the professionals in any organization are most concerned with the first three elements: inputs, processes, and products. The active professional usually takes the ingredients, mixes them properly and at the correct time, and then compares the results with the objectives. The most noticeable and obvious results which we see in any organization are these "products" which are the teacher and learner accomplishments. And as Becky goes through school she will have many such results.

In education there are many of these en-route results (products) because there are quite a few learning activities and experiences that have to be successfully completed before finishing one's education.

ORGANIZATIONAL RESULTS—OUTPUTS

COMPLETING SCHOOL

Becky has many years ahead of her. She will be maturing, growing, and learning both inside and outside of school.

The scene moves ahead thirteen years, and Becky, now eighteen, is getting ready to graduate.

"Mom, I am really excited," she said. "Do you know when I pass my math and art courses I will graduate?"

"Becky, it really seems like just yesterday that I took you to your first day of kindergarten in Mr. Llewelyn's class."

"Do you remember?"

"Sure do."

"There were so many new things. I was really sure that

I was going to be just stupid about everything. All of the other kids seemed so composed and seemed to know just what to do and when to do it."

COMPETENCE

"Remember when you got that poor report card?'" her mother asked, showing perhaps a bit of pain still remaining from that experience.

"I thought I was lucky," Becky replied. "I really goofed off that year. If they were fair, I would have not been promoted into the tenth grade. I really had to work for the last two years to make up for those poor grades."

"Do you think it makes that much difference?" her mom asked.

"Well, if I want to go to college it will. They really look at the grades from high school, and it takes good grades to get into better colleges."

Becky stopped for a moment, looked out at her brother and his young son playing in the front yard, and thought briefly about the fact that her nephew was going to have to go through all of the learning experiences in school that she had gone through. For a flash, Becky thought it was a shame that competence did not come in the genes and thus save every child from reenacting all of the learning experiences. Her flight of fancy ended, and she snapped back into the present.

GRADUATING

"Mom, I'm going to graduate, really."

"How about some of the others, Becky?"

"Sheila is graduating from Tech, Bobby from Roosevelt, and Barbara is getting a certificate to be a beautician this month."

"We are all getting through. You are getting out of high school, and your dad and I are getting our last girl through public school. I am pleased you decided on college, Becky, and I am happy for your friends who are doing other things as well."

OUTPUT

Becky will soon reach the culmination of her years in public school—she is about to graduate. The school has completed its job with her. This completion, called an *educational output*, is the culmination of the school's efforts and Becky's as well. All of the inputs, processes, and products have come to fruition, and Becky graduates. All of the courses passed, the materials mastered, the time spent in libraries and on ball fields and in laboratories and in classes, all the money spent, the materials used, the tests taken and passed, the teachers and aides who spent their time and invested their efforts have added up in this educational output—Becky's graduation.

PUTTING THE ELEMENTS TOGETHER

The term *output* is not very glamorous, but it serves us well, for it cleanly and neatly differentiates between the inputs (the raw materials of the educational system, including goals, teachers, money, buildings, facilities, equipment, learning resources and materials, and the all-important learners), the processes (the ways and means used for delivering learning experiences, the use of materials, the strategies and tools used by teachers, the curriculum, the curriculum guides), the products (the lessons mastered, the courses completed, the tests passed, the grades finished), and the culmination of it all, the diploma or the certificate of completion—the output. The school had done its job, and Becky was graduating.

Included under the term *output* are the number of graduates of an educational agency, the number of completion certificates, the people being licensed—all of the results for which the agency took responsibility for delivery. These outputs are school (or organizational) accomplishments, organizational payoffs and results. Put together all of the organizational efforts and results, and you have the outputs.

But what about the utility of the output? How well did the outputs contribute to Becky and the community?

THE ULTIMATE USEFULNESS OF SCHOOL—OUTCOMES

WHAT'S IT ALL ABOUT?

Let us take another leap forward, this time six years. Becky has completed college, married, and is working with a local computer manufacturer as a statistical analyst. Her daughter is just nine months old, and her husband is working for a local veterinarian, hoping someday to go to veterinary school himself.

EDUCATION IS FOR LIFE

"Boy, mom, sometimes I wonder why I went to school. Most of what I do I didn't learn about in school or in college. Sometimes I feel I have wasted all of those years."

"Oh?"

"Not really, but I wonder sometimes."

"Becky, I do that every now and then myself. I have raised three children, and they all seem to be doing well. I, too, wonder what did I have to go to school for? But then I recall that all I learned has helped to shape me so that I would be a good consumer, get along with others, tolerate differences in ideas and people, learn how to solve problems. Do you know what I mean?"

"I sure do."

"'All of those experiences, I guess, were meant to get us ready for life."

"There were some things that didn't do much good, like learning how to make wooden ashtrays, setting type, and some of those English courses where we studied people I did not know or care about, but all in all, I guess they were trying to get us ready for life."

Becky fell silent. She walked across the room, picked up her baby, rubbed noses with her for a moment, put her down. She flipped her head, and her hair flounced out and settled back, slightly in disarray.

IT IS USEFUL

"There were some really useful things, though. My number facts set the stage for the work I am doing now, and my other skills are the building blocks of working and understanding. I guess by most people's criteria, I am successful. I can make it on my own, both financially and personally, and I get along with most people. I am able to save money, even with high costs. Things will work out. I guess finishing high school and college really did help."

EDUCATION AS AN INTERVENTION

Becky and her mother had discovered the fact—one often overlooked—that schooling is an intervention designed to help people become self-sufficient and able to contribute in the social world outside of school. Becky (and her mom, too) had been prepared, had learned and developed so that they were able to make it on the outside, able to become happy and productive citizens.

When the school system has been successful, when the outputs are negotiable in society, when these external results are seen as useful to the people the system serves, and when there is "audience acceptance," then the *outcomes* are positive. The most basic result for an organization is the impact it has on society. Utility is the key here—are the results of the intervention called "school" (or any other organization for that matter) useful? Are the results more useful than those obtainable through alternative means or from not doing anything at all?

BASIC RESULTS

The outcome of all schooling is indicated by the individual's performance in society. The basic outcome is that all learners will be self-sufficient and able to contribute when they leave the educational system.

The achievement of this outcome is difficult, and it is crucial. It means that all of the inputs, processes, products, outputs, and outcomes have to be synchronized and built one from the other to assure learning success and individual success.

THE ORGANIZATIONAL ELEMENTS MODEL

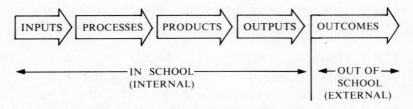

Fig. 2.1 The Organizational Elements Model. Inputs and processes as well as products and outcomes are "internal" since they relate to "in-organizational" activities and results, while outcomes are "external"—they relate to out-of-organizational results.

From this story of Becky and her trip through education, we can now relate everything to organizational efforts (inputs and processes), organizational results (products and outputs) and societal impact (outcomes). The five organizational elements are: inputs, processes, products, outputs and outcomes. Organizational efforts and organizational results are "internal" in that they go on "within" or internal to an organization. Schooling and school efforts are all intended to help people be successful when they leave school and go into the outside world—to be self-sufficient, self-reliant, and not dependent upon others for handouts or charity. Let's take a graphic look at these organizational elements:

The inputs, processes, products, and outputs are all *internal* to the educational system. They are organizational efforts and organizational activities leading to results that are *external* to the school system:

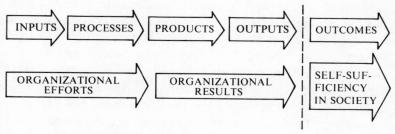

FIG 2.2 The organizational elements model

The school system is an intervention used by a society to prepare its people to survive, be self-sufficient, and contribute in the world of work, social relations, and personal growth and happiness.

In Becky's adventure in public schooling, the school's resources were dedicated to facilitating the growth and learning she required to enable her to function and contribute when she left school. She went to college, and in that case, the higher education experience was another intervention between Becky and her ability to ultimately be self-sufficient and able to contribute when she finished.

USEFULNESS IS THE KEY

While we focus most frequently on the inputs, processes, products, and outputs of schools and schooling, the important part of it all is what it does for learners, such as Becky, when they leave the school. Becky should and did have a number of learning experiences and options presented before she made her life choice.

A NONEDUCATIONAL EXAMPLE

This example of Becky used education as the vehicle for explaining organizational elements (input, process, product, output, outcome), but this model is useful for any intervention area.

A school is a means, an intervention selected by society for helping our learners to become self-sufficient. How about another example outside of the education experience? Let's now take a look at Becky's mother. Her daughter is out on her own now. The scene is three years later, and Becky's mother and father are now divorced. Becky's mother, Barbara, is faced with a new situation—a demand to be self-sufficient, but possessing only the tools from her previous occupation, homemaker. She graduated from college many years before with a degree in liberal studies. She was married right after graduation and never worked outside the home as a paid employee, although she worked as a volunteer for several social service agencies. Her resources from the divorce settlement include the house and one year of alimony. It is now near the end of that year, and her resources are dwindling.

BECKY: Mom, now that you and dad are not together anymore, have you thought about getting a job? I know the money dad gives you is about to run out. What are you planning to do?

BARBARA: I certainly have been thinking about it. (She pauses and wrinkles her brow.) But the only thing I know is homemaking, and now with you gone and with the divorce . . . I have looked at the ads in the paper, but they all say that you have to have experience, and I don't have any. I don't know where the money will come from, and I just don't want to go on welfare.

BECKY: How about going back to school or to a vocational training center? Perhaps they could help you decide what kind of job would be best for you. I heard that the community college has a displaced homemaker center. That's for people who want some help in finding out how to get a job and how to enroll in training programs. There are many women there who have had experiences similar to yours, and maybe they can help you.

BARBARA: That sounds good, but I really think I am too old and set in my ways to learn anything new. Besides, I would have to learn something entirely new. I don't have any skills at all.

BECKY: Now wait a minute! I think you are wrong about that. You did a darned good job of raising me, and I think you were an excellent homemaker. You might have kept the house a bit too clean, but you are good at a lot of things, and many of the skills you have are those you can use on a job.

BARBARA: Like what?

BECKY: You already know how to manage a very complex enterprise—a home and a family. You know how to organize, plan, carry out plans, and change whenever necessary. You have a lot of skills, mom, but you just haven't really taken stock of yourself.

BARBARA: Well . . .

BECKY: How about going to the displaced homemaker center, mom? I know you will find someone to talk with there, and a friend told me that there are several women recently divorced who have gone there for help.

THE COUNSELING PROCESS

Barbara goes to the center with some apprehension and talks with a counselor who really seems to understand her problems. She obviously has dealt with many women like Barbara, and after getting some information, the counselor sits down with Barbara.

COUNSELOR: You are here to get some help and to make some changes in your life. I am here to help you identify your interests, your values—what's important to you—and your skills and abilities. If I am to help you, we'll have to talk these things through and find out what *you* really want.

BARBARA: That's something new for me. I've never really considered what I want. I've always done what's best for the family. And what do you mean about identifying my skills and abilities? All I've ever done is keep house and raise a family.

COUNSELOR: I would like to set some goals with you. Determine where you would like to be in five years, and let me know what you would define as success.

BARBARA: Let me think. (She pauses, looks about the room, starts to speak, stops, and then begins again.) It is really important to me that I be self-sufficient. I know I will get social security and part of a retirement pension, but that will not be enough. I am still young—only forty-eight—and I have a long life ahead of me. I do want to make sure I have enough money to live on and to take care of all my necessities. I hate to talk about money, but it is important that I have enough to survive, and maybe some more above that.

COUNSELOR: Good. That makes sense. Anything else?

BARBARA: I want satisfaction. I want to do something that I feel contributes to others. I like to help people, I am good at relationships, and helping others makes me feel good about myself. I guess some call it psychic income, and that is important to me.

COUNSELOR: Okay, are there any occupational areas you have in mind? Here is a list of helping professions that will be looking for good, concerned people during the next ten to twenty years. (She hands her a list of jobs that includes nursing, social work, teaching, recreation, and so forth.)

BARBARA: I like the idea of being a recreation specialist, and social work appeals to me as well. How do I decide?

COUNSELOR: I would like you to take some time and work through some of these instruments—some call them tests, but they are not—to get some idea of your interests and aptitudes. After that, we can try to match your background, capabilities, interests, and abilities with possible career opportunities. (Barbara comes back several times and works through the materials. Some seem simple to her, some complex, some not terribly sensible, but she does them. She is getting interested in getting back into the mainstream. The counselor has analyzed the results and called Barbara in to talk.)

COUNSELOR: Well, Barbara, you are a pretty interesting person. It seems that your aptitudes and interests lean toward nursing, but you also would be strong in recreation as well. The social worker possibility is a very distant third. Here is why. . . . (Barbara and the counselor go over the data and look at profiles. Barbara gets an explanation of the results and what they mean. They talk, and Barbara thinks about it, comes back, and decides she wants to go the recreation direction. Let's eavesdrop on another discussion.)

COUNSELOR: Here are some ways and means to get trained and hired as a recreation worker. To reach that goal and be certified as hireable by the county, you have to meet the requirements on this sheet I have prepared.

BARBARA: This looks good. How do I start?

COUNSELOR: There is a course of study here at the college, and here are some part-time jobs you can get which will help you in the certification test when it is scheduled.

BARBARA: Great. Let's sign me up!

Barbara, having had her interests and characteristics appraised, is embarking upon a new life. She enters the training program, masters the material, and passes all of her courses. She also works and gets letters of accomplishment to show that she has had experience in the recreation field.

The test for recreation specialist is scheduled, and Barbara takes it and passes it. She is now on a register for a job, and while she is working part-time at the college girls' swimming pool, she is notified of a job that is available at the city playground as a worker in retired persons' activities. She is interviewed, gets the job, and is now financially self-sufficient. She is making enough money to live on, saves a bit, is working on her retirement benefits through savings and city contributions, and is delighted with her job. Once a displaced homemaker, Barbara is now employed and contributing.

THE ORGANIZATIONAL ELEMENTS AND BARBARA

As we went through this fictional case study, you might have noticed that there were the same elements working as in the story of Becky. Let's take a look.

OUTCOME

Barbara wanted to be, and now is, self-sufficient. She requires no money from other sources, and can pay all of her bills. She is saving for the future and has a retirement plan developing. She is also happy in her new role and her job.

OUTPUT

Barbara had to be certified as a recreation specialist, and she had to pass an examination. The output for her was this completion—all of her courses and her work, all of her experiences and mastery were certified. This is the point where she enters society.

PRODUCT

Completing the courses successfully, satisfactorily completing related training jobs, doing all of the tasks that were required to get Barbara from being a displaced homemaker to certification—all of these are the products.

PROCESSES

The pathway and options Barbara chose—classes to be taken, jobs to be satisfactorily performed—were all the processes used by Barbara to achieve the products. These were the ways and means used to get Barbara trained and competent.

INPUTS

When the counselor asked Barbara to take some inventories and assessed her interests and capabilities, the inputs were being determined. These were the starting conditions. Other inputs included Barbara's goals and desires, the requirements for the occupation she wanted, and the time and money to complete her training and become employed.

RELATING CHAPTER ONE
AND CHAPTER TWO

The first chapter defined and described tools and techniques that were central to evaluation: goals, objectives, needs, needs assessment, planning, evaluation, testing, and measurement. The second chapter suggested various places within and external to organizations where these tools might be useful. One could plan the achievement of any one of the organizational elements, or could plan to achieve useful results from all of the elements so that a total organization would have useful outcomes.

Needs assessment or determination of gaps in results could be accomplished for any one element or any combination of the elements.

And so, too, could we set goals and objectives for each or any combination, and we could likewise gather data (test), and measure (compare results against some useful standards), for any one or a combination of the organizational elements. And finally, we could evaluate within any one of the elements or for any combination of the elements.

We could determine the extent to which we accomplished what we set out to accomplish and also determine if what we did accomplish was of value: valuation and evaluation.

Chapter 1 presented tools useful for evaluation, and Chapter 2 provided an overall framework for organizational activities, results, and accomplishments in which these tools could be usefully employed.

Chapter 1 presented tools, and Chapter 2 explained environments for use of the tools.

Now that we have set the stage the next chapter will go into detail about the most basic planning and direction-finding tools—needs assessment.

KEY POINTS

- In order to accomplish something, we must use ingredients such as resources, people, facilities, and goals and objectives. These ingredients and resources are called "inputs."
- The manner in which the ingredients are orchestrated and staged, the methods and means by which we put ingredients to work, are called "processes."
- When our ingredients and processes are completed, we get results, called "products." Examples of products are completed courses (teacher accomplishments and learner accomplishments), or the findings from a routine brain scan and blood chemistry analysis.
- When all of the products are combined in a useful and meaningful manner, they then represent the organizational accomplishments, called "outputs." Outputs might include graduates from a junior college, patients discharged as healthy from a hospital, or counselees who are "together" enough to go out from therapy and function completely on their own.
- But what about the "leavers"?—those graduating or discharged? What is the impact of these outputs in and

for society? Do the discharged patients maintain their health, or do they go back to old habits and end up back at the hospital, or back into counseling? Do junior college graduates end up on relief or unemployment, or do they earn their own way until retirement? The impact of the outputs in society is labeled "outcome."

• Regardless of the organization, regardless of where it works in our society, these elements describe the elements which are important, and further, they describe how they relate to each other.

Selected References

1. Kaufman, R. *Educational System Planning*. Englewood Cliffs, N.J.: Prentice-Hall, 1972.
2. Kaufman, R. *Identifying and Solving Problems: A System Approach*. 2nd ed. La Jolla, Calif.: University Associates Publishers, 1979.
3. Kaufman, R., and Carron, A. S. "Utility and Self-Sufficiency in the Selection of Educational Alternatives." Occasional Paper No. 8. Tallahassee: Center for Needs Assessment and Planning, Learning Systems Institute, Florida State University, January 1979.
4. Kaufman, R., and English, F. W. *Needs Assessment: Concept and Application*. Englewood Cliffs, N.J.: Educational Technology Publications, 1979.

3
EVALUATION AND NEEDS ASSESSMENT

Evaluation, needs assessment, goal-setting, and planning are all linked: 1) Needs assessment is the determination of where one is and where one should be. 2) Planning is the determination of what functions are to be performed to get from where one is to where one should be. 3) Goals and objectives are set to specify precisely where one hopes to go. 4) Evaluation is the determination of the gaps that exist between what you set out to accomplish and what you have accomplished.

Most practitioners are busy, overloaded with work. Doing a needs assessment might seem to be an additional burden when doing evaluation, but in spite of this, it is worth considering. The only time you do not have to conduct a needs assessment is that time when you are sure that the goals and objectives for your organization and/or program are complete, correct, valid, and useful. If you are not certain of their appropriateness, then needs assessment will better assure that valuable time will not be wasted. If you think you are busy now, imagine what your load might get to be if it turns out that you have been evaluating the wrong things or that your organization has been doing less-than-useful things! Needs assessment (actually there are several varieties to choose among) is a tool to make sure of where you are going and to further justify that direction. After determining if the goals and objectives are correct, the evaluation may continue—with confidence.

NEEDS ARE GAPS

When you are planning to get from one place to another, it helps to know several things:

- Where you are now—exactly?
- Where do you want to be—exactly?
- Why do you want to be there?

It makes simple sense to determine exactly where you are now, where you want to go, and why you want to go there. A need is the gap between where one is and where one wants to be. It is the discrepancy between current results and desired results. A need shows the polar positions of "what is" and "what should be" in terms of outcomes. It is similar to the major supports of a bridge across a chasm; each support is on one side of the chasm. If we want to get from one side to the other, then we define our current position, determine our required position, and then "anchor" these before building the passageway. Actually, we should also first determine if we should go from one side of the chasm to the other: is the trip really necessary?

Needs are identified and documented as part of comprehensive planning and before implementation, evaluation, and revision.

Needs assessment is the process of determining gaps between "what is" and "what should be," placing the gaps in priority order, and selecting gaps of the highest priority for resolution. Needs, then, are gaps; needs assessment is the formal process for identifying, justifying, and then selecting needs for closure.

Some semantics. Need is a badly abused word. There have even been court cases involving the word and its vague and contradictory usage by people and legislatures. While it might seem to be presumptuous or even crass, we are offering a unique use of *need* as *a gap between current results* (or, ideally, *outcomes*) *and desired results* (also, ideally, *outcomes*). In this usage, *need* is a noun, not a verb. Quibbling? It might sound so, but we are interested in getting the results we want to get, and we don't want to get off the target because of misunderstandings or because we selected the wrong goals and objectives. If we use a descriptive word that leads us in the wrong direction, then the word should be replaced. Or precisely defined and used. And so it is with the word *need*; we want to use it in a very specific way, a way that is different from the conventional wisdom of everyday language. We want to use it to mean *a gap in results*, not a gap in inputs, processes, or solutions.

When *need* is used as a noun we are discussing gaps in results, not gaps in methods. Let's examine this difference and see where it leads us. Here is a hypothetical speech by a principal to a faculty:

> *Today we are interested in a new reading program. We* need *a reading program to help learners read better. We* need *a new reading program because the scores on the statewide tests are down—the third lowest in the county. Thus we are going to assess the* need *for a new reading program, and then we are going to select the new JDK program materials.*

Now, let's examine this statement. In it, it is stated with no *ifs, ands,* or *buts* that the reading program is *"needed."* A new reading program is a means, a solution, a possible means to an end to accomplish higher reading scores and perhaps improve reading skills and abilities. The focus of this dialogue, from the beginning, was on means—a new reading program—and not on results—improvement of reading skills and abilities. By using *need* as a verb, the speaker has leaped right over the gaps in results (learners unable to survive and perform because of inability to encode, decode, and process symbolic information, such as written words) into "thus we are going to assess the *need* for a new reading program, and then we are going to select the new JDK program materials."

The possible trap is leaping right to solutions before we have verified the gap in results and used that verified gap to identify different possible ways and means of closing the gap. (It is interesting to notice that *if* a new reading program were to be selected, an unwary evaluator could simply compare the reading program objectives with reading performance, and the resulting evaluation data would not determine the utility of the results. Perhaps the reading program, in this hypothetical example, was developed based upon the reading characteristics of suburban learners and the group using it consists of inner city learners. In this case, different meanings might be inferred by this target group from the reading materials than those intended.)

As an example of this hypothetical situation, the problem that gave rise to the principal selecting the new reading program might actually have been the result of several possible factors: invalid state test of reading, nonfunctional reading objectives and delivery, or a reading program that is not useful to the learners, to name a few. It might have been that the reading program was useful, but by using the word *need* as a verb, the speaker implied that a new program was *needed*. A solution was selected *before* the problem was identified and justified!

Let's try one more hypothetical case:

The Bloxham Swamp Counseling Center needs *more money because the state's influx of veterans and retired people has increased the case load 70 percent in the last year, the buildings are in poor repair, and counselors' salaries are much too low.*

This statement could have been made by the district director, the advisory board president, or the head of the social services council. By inference, the ills of the Bloxham Swamp Counseling Center are going to be solved by more money. Money is *inferred* to be the solution. But what's the problem? It is not the money that is important, by itself, but it is what the money can purchase—as a means to an end— and this is critical. If the money is not spent wisely or well, then next year the center is likely to have the same problems as it has this year. Thus, the "need" for money was used as a reason to jump into the collection and use of money before the actual gap was identified and justified, probably because, among other things, the objectives of the center were not linked to the outcome—self-sufficiency and contribution outside the center. Resources and techniques should be directed toward allowing clients to be coping, self-sufficient people, at the very least.

Means and ends (again). This confusion between means and ends is almost universal in our culture. We elect to seek more money before we know what we can productively use the money to achieve. We argue about teacher salaries, number of administrators, hours of nursing care, accountability, phonics; on and on we argue about means, but we rarely talk about outcomes.

We suggest that learning to distinguish between means and ends is critical in successful planning and evaluating.

Evaluation often leads one into asking not only "What happened?" but also "What should have happened?" If you know that most people, educators included, focus on means and not ends, then you can have some pretty good insights into why promised programs and projects did not "pay off" the way everyone expected.

In asking you not to use the word *need* as a verb (or in a verb sense), we are trying to get you to act upon the fact that there is a difference between means and ends—between the gaps in results and the means by which we might achieve gap closure. The point is to learn not to confuse the ends (closing the gap and meeting the *need*) with the means (the how-to-do-its) that we choose to try to produce useful results.

NEEDS ASSESSMENT

Needs assessment is a process used to define and rank gaps. We suggest that a needs assessment can take many useful forms but the most fundamental one will identify, document, and justify gaps in outcomes.

Following is a discussion of two major types of needs assessments, both of which can be useful in revealing gaps to you and your organization. In selecting one you should be aware that the only difference between them is the question to be addressed. Let's take a closer look.

Needs assessments (as well as planning) can be conveniently grouped into two general categories:
- EXTERNAL NEEDS ASSESSMENT
- INTERNAL NEEDS ASSESSMENT

The external variety looks at gaps between outcomes, while the internal variety seeks to identify gaps in inputs, or process, or products, or outputs.

Remember from Chapter 2 that the elements of education could be related to organizational efforts and organizational results (internal), and these in turn yield societal impact (external).

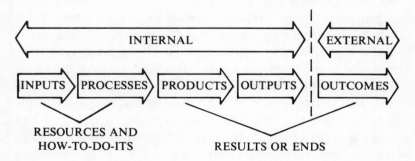

Figure 3-1. The organizational elements: some deal with results, and some relate to resources and methods-means.

There are several types of internal needs assessment models, and there is only one external mode.

Let us look at each category. First the external variety.

EXTERNAL NEEDS ASSESSMENT

In using an external needs assessment we are addressing the following question:

What are the requirements for self-sufficiency, self-reliance, and contribution in today's and tomorrow's world, regardless of how we help and allow our citizens to achieve those requirements?

In order to answer this question, we have to determine two poles: "what is" and "what should be" in terms of outcomes—easy to ask, but more difficult to answer.

In asking this question, we are seeking to determine what skills, knowledge, and yes, attitudes will be required to achieve self-sufficiency and contribution in today's and tomorrow's world and what are the gaps between our current skills, knowledge, and attitudes (SKAs) and the required ones.

To take this approach is to move from possible "cosmetic" change to deep change. This approach brings into question the usefulness and utility of current ways of doing things and even the current goals and objectives of our organizations. (Beware! Questioning an organization's goals can be disturbing to others in that organization, especially if those people are more concerned about preserving their territory and power than they are about making the organization useful to society.)

This external type of needs assessment is critical if one is to do more than just take what is currently going on and make it more efficient. It moves to assure that our organizational and personal efforts are not only successful in meeting objectives, but that we are responsive and responsible for improving our world by assuring the usefulness of the objectives.

Determine what should be. This is the most difficult question—what should be. It requires us to take a risk and look into the future. It requires us to look at the skills, knowledge, and attitudes that will be necessary for self-sufficiency and contribution. It asks us to move from looking only at input, process, product, and output to looking also at outcomes. It also requires us to be somewhat inductive in our thinking and to look at a world of possibilities and probabilities, not just a world of current results.

There are a number of sources for determining possible "futures" including formal studies of the future. A library should be able to supply these. One indicator of self-sufficiency (or survival) requirements (for now and the future) may be found in an economic utility model, which states that the basic, minimum (not maximum), fundamental indicator for the success of any societal endeavor such as education is this:

> *By the time the individual legally exits from the agency, she or he will be at a self-sufficiency point or beyond.*

This states that after any intervention, any organizational effort or activity or program, those impacted will be at a self-sufficiency point or beyond in society.

One way of measuring this self-sufficiency point is through the use of an *indicator**—money. If, after participating in a program, individuals have incomes equal to or greater than their expenses, then this is an indicator that they are at the point of self-sufficiency or beyond.

---

*An indicator is an index which, by agreement, represents a total array of happenings. It is an agreed-upon, often convenient reduction of the complexity of our real world.

We could derive detailed indicators of this, for example, by determining an intended target group's income/expense ratios and by determining (correcting for inflation, and so on) what will be required in the future. The gap between current and future self-sufficiency/contribution levels could be used to show the external *need*—the gap between current outcomes and desired outcomes.

Frequently, these data may be obtained from the federal, state, or local department of commerce. Once derived, this level will serve as a *standard*, or pattern, against which possible outputs, products, processes, and inputs may be considered and used or not used. If input, process, product, or output will not change the outcome—the level of self-sufficiency and contribution—of the individuals to be affected, why should we choose that element? The only instance where one would want to choose such an internal element occurs when one is convinced that there is an indirect relationship that is not currently provable and when one is willing to risk the expenditure of inputs anyway, or when one wishes to have the luxury of utilizing such resources and having the results considered worthy for their own sake.

To do an external needs assessment, then, one simply has to determine the gaps between current levels of self-sufficiency and contribution (as indicated by the ratio of income to outgo by the target recipients) and use these as the overall objective—to close the gaps between current levels and required levels. Once these external criteria are set (or once one is willing to assume that outcomes will be achieved that will later be evaluated as worthwhile), then the internal varieties of needs assessment modes become useful.*

---

* Feeling overworked with new words and "jargon"? Jargon is a word someone else uses that we do not or will not understand.

INTERNAL NEEDS ASSESSMENT

When we are concerned with gaps relating to inputs, processes, products, and outputs, we are looking at variables *internal* to an organization. We are looking at gaps between what is and what should be for organizational efforts and organizational results.

There are two varieties of organizational efforts:
Inputs
Processes

There are two varieties of organizational results:
Products
Outputs

For simplicity, we suggest that, in conducting an internal needs assessment, we may look at gaps between current internal factors and desired internal factors. (Actually, since a need is a gap in results, those discrepancy analyses concerned with inputs and processes are "quasi-needs assessments." Needs assessments properly relate to gaps in results.)

Here are some questions that could be answered by internal needs assessments:

What are the gaps between current organizational goals and policies and functional ones?

What are the gaps between the outputs we are now achieving and outputs that would be more useful?

These relate, of course, to outputs. What about those other internal elements?

Which of the current methods are most cost-effective?

Are these methods the most economical and effective, or are there others that would be better?

These relate to products.

Now for needs assessments (really quasi-needs assessments) for the other organizational elements that are internal:

How are the methods working as compared to the way in which they are supposed to work?

Are all of the methods and materials working where they are supposed to be and when they are supposed to be?

Were the materials of the quality they were advertised as being?

Finally, for inputs:

Did the learners have the characteristics that were identified for them?

Was the budget correct or deficient?

Were the goals and objectives understandable?

THE NEEDS ASSESSMENT STEPS

Regardless of the needs assessment mode you select—external or internal—there will be a number of common steps:

1. *Identify what is.* Collect data, reduce and summarize the data. Categories to be included will be determined by
    A. the needs assessment mode selected, and
    B. the focus of the assessment.

If the mode is external, then the focus will be society and individual and collective self-sufficiency and contribution; if it is the assessment only of a new training procedure, then it will revolve around only inputs, processes, and products.

2. *Identify what should be.* This step is the same as the previous one with the inclusion of looking at future trends and possible future situations.

Make sure that the statements of what is and what should be are in performance terms that are ideally measurable on an interval or ratio scale (see Chapter 1).

3. *Make a needs assessment matrix.* This will show what is and what should be for the three partners:

A. Learners (recipients of any intervention),
B. Implementers (those responsible for any intervention), and
C. Society/community (those who support any intervention and receive those who are the recipients).

This partnership is important to assure that all perspectives and values will be included in the planning, doing, and evaluation.

The matrix may be composed in this format:

PARTNER	WHAT IS	WHAT SHOULD BE
Recipients		
Implementers		
Society/community		

Fill in the information, making sure that it relates actual and required conditions and that they are measurable on an interval or ratio scale.

Each "what is" does not have to have a parallel "what should be." There are many "what is" statements that merely document the starting conditions, such as age, sex, number of teachers, current law.

4. *Reconcile any differences between the partners that might show up in the needs assessment matrix.*

This can frequently be accomplished by making each partner deal with outcomes (or at least outputs), rather than inputs or processes. (This might sound too simple, but it works. The confusion between means and ends can be quickly seen as the culprit in many disagreements.)

Hypothetical example:

PARTNER	WHAT IS	WHAT SHOULD BE
Recipients	78% of graduates do get and keep jobs. Schoolwork is not exciting enough so that people want to come to school (30% truancy).	At least 90% of graduates get and keep jobs. Truancy rate no more than 5%. Reading mastery accomplished in 96% of learners.
Implementers	Not all teachers can teach reading (only 68% certified in reading). Teachers in physical jeopardy (11% were assaulted last year).	Assault rate no more than 1% per year.
Society/community	Crime rate is too high (arrest rate is 1 in 7 citizens). Job applicants cannot read (56% cannot fill out a job application correctly).	Crime rate no more than 1 arrest per 100. At least 96% of all job applicants can correctly fill out job application forms.

Figure 3-2. A hypothetical example of a needs assessment summary matrix. Note that not all statements are complete, are stated on an ordinal or interval or ratio scale of measurement, or relate to outcomes. Subsequent development using this matrix would "shape" toward meeting the criteria of outcome statements and statements that are objectives (not just goals).

5. *List the needs.* This is a simple process of taking all of the gaps identified and making a list. Make sure they are all measurable on an interval or ratio scale.

Hypothetical listing of a first cut at needs based on the needs assessment matrix on page 64, figure 3.2, are:

78% of graduates do get and keep jobs currently, and this should be increased to at least 90%.

Current truancy rate is 30% and should be reduced to no more than 5%.

68% of teachers certified in reading currently, and there should be enough teacher competency in facilitating learning to assure that at least 96% of all learners can be certified as having minimal reading competency.

11% of all teachers in the system were assaulted last year, and this should be reduced to no more than 1% next year.

6. *Place the needs in priority order*. This may be done in a variety of ways.

One suggested criterion is to ask each of the partners (or their representatives) to sort the listed needs in priority order on the basis of asking the dual question, "What does it cost to meet the need, and what will it cost to ignore the need?"

7. *Select the needs for action*. Usually this is easily done on the basis of the resources (inputs) available.

STEPS IN NEEDS ASSESSMENT— GETTING READY

The following diagram shows the sequence of steps that you might consider in conducting a needs assessment. The entry point to planning needs assessment and evaluation is the point at which you (or your organization) decide to plan. Thus figure 3.3 starts at that point.

Notice that in the diagram there are several places where a choice may be selected. The riskiest choice is the one where you might decide that the focus of the existing goals and objectives is valid and useful. While this choice is a convenient one, it usually is not substantiative.

In both cases the terminal place for your analysis will be going on to consideration of appropriate evaluation models and tools.

DECIDE TO EVALUATE

Put existing goals and objectives into measurable terms (ordinal or interval measures) (Chapter 1, page 10)

Determine focus of goals and objectives (page 42)

> outcomes
> outputs
> products
> process(es)
> inputs

Determine if you are sure the focus of given goals and objectives is valid and useful

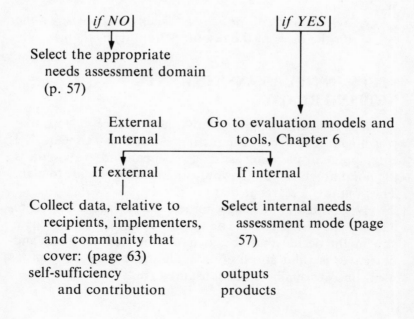

|if NO|

Select the appropriate
needs assessment domain
(p. 57)

External
Internal

If external
|
Collect data, relative to
recipients, implementers,
and community that
cover: (page 63)
self-sufficiency
and contribution

|if YES|

Go to evaluation models and
tools, Chapter 6

If internal

Select internal needs
assessment mode (page
57)

outputs
products

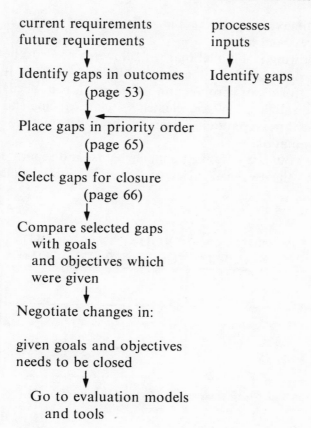

current requirements   processes
future requirements   inputs

Identify gaps in outcomes   Identify gaps
        (page 53)

Place gaps in priority order
        (page 65)

Select gaps for closure
        (page 66)

Compare selected gaps
    with goals
    and objectives which
    were given

Negotiate changes in:

given goals and objectives
needs to be closed

    Go to evaluation models
        and tools

Figure 3.3. The general steps in needs assessment

AN OPERATIONAL PROCESS FOR ASSESSING NEEDS FOR ALL OF THE ORGANIZATIONAL ELEMENTS

In any of the five organizational elements, a need may be identified as a gap between current and required results.

Most organizational efforts revolve around inputs and processes, and rarely do we consider the implications of these "early" elements for organizational results and organizational impacts on society. But these organizational results and impacts may make the difference between our internal success and failure.

The following is a model that will allow for needs to be identified *in* and *for* all of the organizational elements. It suggests a "flow" or progression of steps for a needs assessment through all of the elements, relates them, and then provides for a continuing basis for both needs assessment and evaluation.

First, lay out the organizational elements, and separate each one for the two categories of "what is" and "what should be":

	INPUTS	PRO-CESSES	PROD-UCTS	OUT-PUTS	OUT-COMES
WHAT IS					
WHAT SHOULD BE					

Figure 3.4. The Basic Needs Assessment and Evaluation Matrix

Next, start focusing your attention and needs assessment efforts on the first and most available data area, "what is," for inputs. Collect and list these data (No. 1 in the *following* figure 3.5), and then move on to the next data collection job for "processes" (No. 2). Continue in this manner, collecting and listing "what is" data through all of the remaining organizational elements (3, 4, and 5).

Now, turn the corner and determine "what should be" for outcomes (6), and next continue down the elements deriving, in turn, the "what should be" for each (7, 8, 9, and 10).

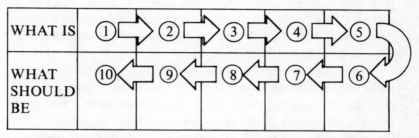

Figure 3.5. The steps for conducting both external and internal needs assessments using the organizational elements model. The numbers indicate the sequence suggested for initiating the needs assessment.

Evaluation may deal with any or all of these organizational elements and the questions to which they give rise.

"What do you want to know?" is the basic guide to planning and doing an evaluation.

After completing this data collection of "what is" and "what should be" for each of the organizational elements, then gaps between each one (see the dark arrows in figure 3.6) may be determined. The result of this process will be the identification of needs for each of the organizational elements.

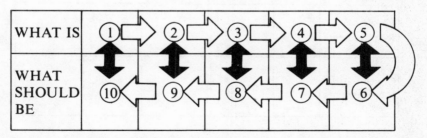

Figure 3.6. The steps for conducting an internal and external needs assessment which shows both the steps and the various places to identify gaps between "what is" and "what should be" for each of the elements.

A needs assessment is concerned with both change and continuation. It is easy to assume that needs assessment, planning, and evaluation are only concerned with change. If it is to be useful, a needs assessment process and an evaluation model will identify what might be usefully continued as well as what should be changed.

In figure 3.6 the processes of moving along the organizational elements from "what is" through input, process, product, output and outcome is first accomplished; and then you do the "backward" analysis for "what should be" for the elements, moving from outcome to output, to product, process, and input. After the two dimensions of "what is" and "what should be" have been identified, and the gaps documented, we list two things for each of the elements:

- change requirements
- continuation requirements.

The format would thus be:

INPUT PROCESS PRODUCT OUTPUT OUTCOME

	INPUT	PROCESS	PRODUCT	OUTPUT	OUTCOME
WHAT IS					
WHAT SHOULD BE					
Change Requirements					
Continuation Requirements					

Figure 3.7. The organizational elements model where a needs assessment has been accomplished, and which stipulates that there be a listing of both requirements for change as well as listing those requirements for maintenance—continuing that which is currently working well.

By including the "continuation requirements," it will be clear to both the planner and those involved in the planning that both changes and maintaining what is currently working are foci of needs assessment, planning, and evaluation.

NEEDS ASSESSMENT, CHANGE, MAINTENANCE, AND EVALUATION

Using these organizational elements, and identifying needs and the resulting requirements for changing what should be changed and keeping what is working well, the professional interventionist has to choose what will meet the needs and close the gaps, or keep the gaps closed. One should either change that which is going on, or keep doing that which is now working.

Based upon this information, the intervention specialist may list possible interventions (figure 3.8) for each or several of the organizational elements, and then selects the interventions, also shown in figure 3.8.

Thus, the organizational elements have been used to identify "what is" and "what should be" for each of the elements (figure 3.4); have shown the order for doing a needs assessment (figure 3.5); shown how one may harvest the needs for each of the elements (figure 3.6); noted both change and continuation requirements for each of the organizational elements (figure 3.7); and noted that one should consider possible interventions and then select the most effective and efficient ones to meet the needs (figure 3.8).Now for linking these models with evaluation.

Evaluation is a process for determining if we have in fact accomplished that which we set out to accomplish and determining whether or not the interventions were worth doing.

Using the same organizational elements model one may recycle through the model to determine if the gaps previously identified are now reduced or eliminated. This "recycling"

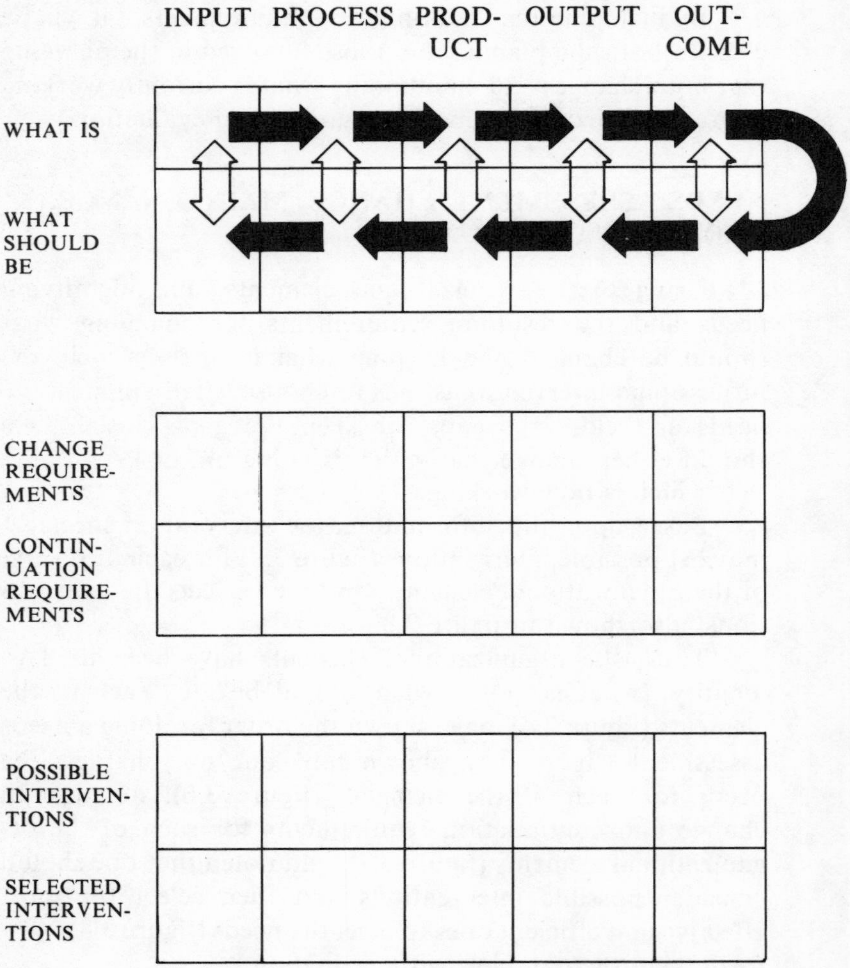

FIGURE 3.8. After the listing of what should be continued and what should be maintained, possible interventions are identified. Next, based upon the possible ways to change what should be changed, and continuing what should be maintained, the interventions to be used are selected. After this, implementation may begin. The interventions will lead to products, outputs, and outcomes.

is shown in figure 3.9 in broken lines. By so doing, one simply re-enters the model at "what is" and examines the extent to which the gap between "what is" and "what should be" for each of the elements has met expectations.

One further evaluation possibility is to relate the elements one to the other to determine if there has been a useful linkage between adjacent organizational elements. For instance, one could determine the linkage between inputs (dollars, trained licensed nurses, and hospital policy and regulations) and the processes delivered (home care, personal health education, professional staff development) to see if the two were productively complementary, or if there were "mismatches" (not enough money for the staff development, current policy did not allow for home care delivery, etc.).

Thus, evaluation may examine the relationship between any of the organizational elements. The most conventional evaluation relationships are *between* adjacent "what is" and "what should be" elements, but there also may be examinations of adjacent elements *within* "what is" and "what should be." It all depends on what questions you want answers to!

Again, the dotted lines in figure 3.9 show the several evaluation possibilities.

Finally, this resulting evaluation data may serve as the basis for another needs assessment. One simply takes the new data base resulting from the evaluation, uses it as a new "what is" and then repeats the same procedures similar to what was previously accomplished and shown in figures 3.5, 3.6, 3.7 and 3.8.

Needs assessment and evaluation, then, are continuing processes and should be undertaken anytime change is possible or required. "One-shot" needs assessments and evaluations assume a static world, an assumption which is very risky to make.

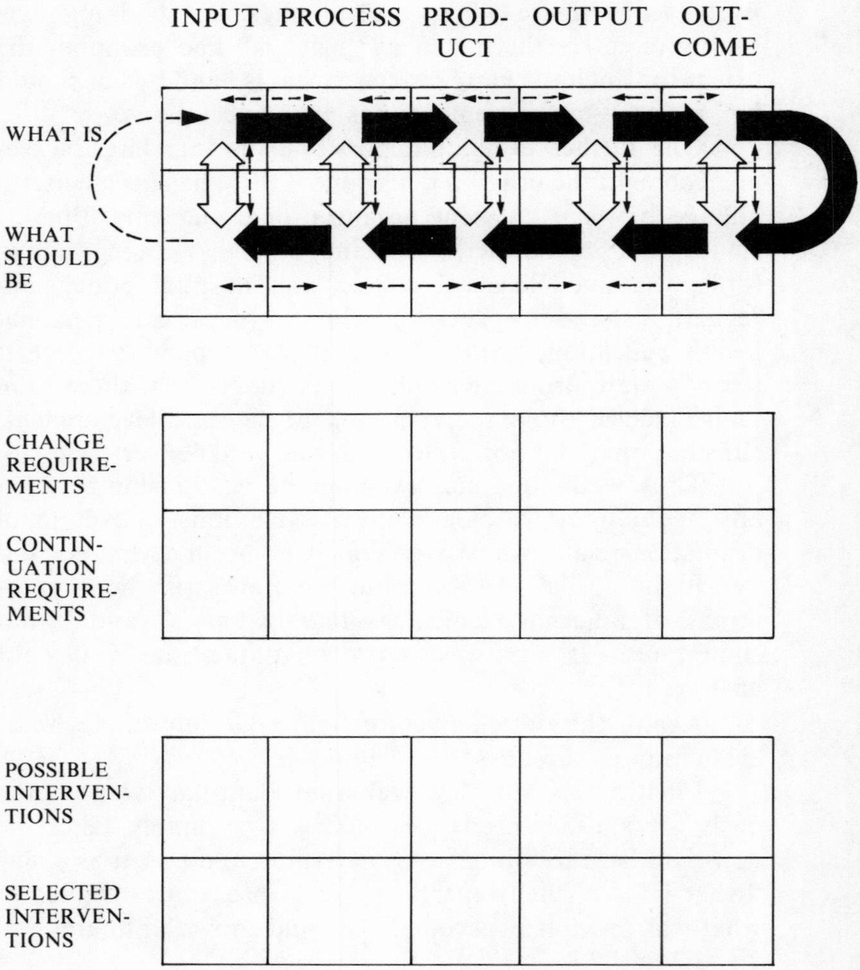

FIGURE 3.9. Evaluation is the process of determining if we accomplished what we set out to accomplish. Evaluation is shown here with the broken arrows, and shows that it consists of determining the extent to which gaps were closed, and which required continuation results are to be maintained, for *each* of the organizational elements. A new needs assessment should be begun with this new data base resulting from the evaluation and determination of the new "what is" for each of the organizational elements.

KEY POINTS

- Needs assessment can help you to determine new goals and objectives as well as to confirm or replace existing ones.
- Knowing where you are going and having confidence in the destination can save you time and effort.
- Needs serve as the base for planning, doing, and evaluating.
- *Needs*, as that term is used here, are gaps. The most fundamental type of need refers to human survival and contribution and thus relates to outcomes.
- Needs assessments may be broken into two overarching types: external and internal.
- External needs assessment deals with outcomes. Internal needs assessment deals with outputs, products, and quasi-needs assessments deal with processes, and inputs.
- Each type of needs assessment is designed to answer different questions.
- A needs assessment may be accomplished for any one, or any combination of, the organizational elements. One identifies the gaps between "what is" and "what should be."
- A sequence which might be used to conduct a needs assessment including all of the elements, would be to move from a determination of "what is" for each of the elements—moving from input through process, product, outputs, and outcome—and then determining next "what should be" for outcome, then through output to product, process and finally input. Given these data, then the gaps between each element are determined.
- Based upon the gaps in any one or a combination of, the organizational elements, one will next determine:
  —Change requirements
  —Maintenance requirements (those things to be maintained or continued) and then one is ready for the

planning of what should be accomplished by the organization.
- Given the change and maintenance requirements, the interventionist is now able to list:
  —Possible methods and means to achieve each set of requirements, and then
  —The most effective and efficient methods—means to do each.
- Evaluation is seen as a logical extension of this process— one may finally compare, after the interventions have been used and data collected—that which was intended for each of the organizational elements with that which was actually accomplished.
- The organizational elements model may be used to understand and relate needs assessment and evaluation. These are different but related.

Selected References

1. Kaufman, R. *Educational System Planning.* Englewood Cliffs, N.J.: Prentice-Hall, 1972.
2. Kaufman, R. *Identifying and Solving Problems: A System Approach.* 2nd Ed. La Jolla, Calif. University Associates Publishers, 1979.
3. Lessinger, L.M., and Gillis, D. *Teaching as a Performing Art.* Dallas: Crescendo Pubs., 1977.
4. Kaufman, R., and English, F.W. *Needs Assessment: Concept and Application.* Englewood Cliffs, N.J.: Educational Technology Publications, 1979.
5. Mager, R.F. *Preparing Instructional Objectives.* 2nd ed. Belmont, Calif.: Fearon, 1975.
6. Popham, W.J. *Selecting Appropriate Educational Objectives.* Los Angeles: Vimcet Associates, 1967.
7. Kibler, R.J., and Bassett, R.E. "Writing Performance Objectives." in *Instructional Design, Principles*

and Applications, edited by L.J. Briggs. Englewood Cliffs, N.J.: Educational Technology Publications, 1977.

8. Mager, R.F., and Pipe, P. *Criterion Referenced Instruction: Analysis, Design, and Implementation:* Participant Manual. Los Altos Hill, Calif.: Mager, 1976.

9. Kaufman, R., and Carron, A.S. "Utility and Self-Sufficiency in the Selection of Educational Alternatives." Occasional Paper No. 8. Tallahassee: Center for Needs Assessment and Planning, Learning Systems Institute, Florida State University, January 1979.

10. Reusch, J. *Knowledge in Action: Communication, Social Operations, and Management.* New York: Aronson, 1975.

11. Kaufman, R. "Beyond Performance and Instruction." *NSPI Journal,* December 1979.

12. Flanders, N.A. *Analyzing Teacher Behavior.* Reading, Mass.: Addison-Wesley, 1970.

13. Provus, M. *Discrepancy Evaluation.* Berkeley, Calif.: McCutchan, 1972.

14. Scriven, M. *The Methodology of Evaluation.* AERA Monograph Series on Curriculum Evaluation. Chicago: Rand McNally, 1967.

15. Scriven, M. and Roth, J. "Needs Assessment: Concept and Practice." *New Directions for Program Evaluation* I (Spring 1978).

16. Supreme Court of Florida, No. 53, 384, Florida Home Builders Association, et al., Appellants, versus Division of Labor, Bureau of Apprenticeship, Appelles, January 25, 1979.

4
NEEDS ASSESSMENT, PLANNING, AND GOAL SETTING

Needs assessment is the first and most indispensable step in any plan to improve a learning program or institution. A plan can be defined as either a comprehensive set of goals and the means for achieving them or as the organized steps we take in sequence to achieve a goal *once that goal has been chosen.*

If we use the word *plan* in the comprehensive sense, needs assessment would be the first step in that process. If we view *plan* as dealing only with the means, or organized program, to close the gaps revealed a by needs assessment, then the picture is a bit different. In that case, we start with existing goals and objectives; then we plan ways to achieve them.

PLANNING

Planning is used when you want to get from where you are to someplace else—on purpose. When you do not care about the results, why bother to plan?

We suggest a simple but powerful planning model that is useful no matter where you start your planning. Of course,we suggest that planning start at the external level—with determination of gaps between what is and what should be in terms of self-sufficiency, but the following planning model can be used for that and for different starting places.

A PLANNING MODEL

We have seen that organizational efforts yield organizational results, and if we are judicious in our selection of organizational resources and efforts, we will get societal results that will lead to individual and collective self-sufficiency. The system approach process is designed to start with the determination of self-sufficiency requirements and build the bridge between current levels and required levels. *The steps to good planning*:

• Identify the problem based upon needs. This step requires that we determine external needs, place the needs in priority order (usually on the basis of what it costs to meet the needs versus what it costs to ignore the needs), and select the need(s) of highest priority for resolution. A need selected for resolution is called a *problem*.

• Determine solution requirements and identify solution alternatives. On the basis of the gaps between what is and what should be, we determine the detailed requirements (identical to objectives) necessary to get from where we are to where we want to be. We list these requirements (including specifications for inputs, processes, products, and outputs) and then identify—without selecting—possible how-to-do-its for meeting the individual and collective requirements. When no methods-means exist for achieving one or more objectives, then there is a constraint, and one either has to invent a new method-means or has to stop.

This second planning step actually determines all of the requirements for problem resolution, identifies possible ways and means for achieving these requirements, and provides a listing for the planner of feasible "whats" to be accomplished along with possible how-to-do-its.

These first two steps are concerned with determining and *justifying* what is to be done and with determining what is available to get the "whats" accomplished; the balance of the model is concerned with getting the "whats" accomplished.

• Select solution strategies from among alternatives. Based upon the requirements for problem resolution and the list of possible how-to-do-its, the most effective and efficient methods and means are selected.

• Implement selected methods and means. Here is the "doing" part of planning and implementation. We use and manage the inputs and processes selected to get the objectives accomplished. During implementation we get products, outputs, and outcomes accomplished. This is the heart of successful activity, but it is usually most successful when the previous steps are accomplished first!

• Determine performance effectiveness. Here is "summative" evaluation. Based upon the needs identified in the first step, the detailed requirements in the second one, the selection of alternative methods-means in the third, and the implementation in the fourth, we check to see which objectives have been achieved and which have not. Then we make a list of that which should be continued and that which should be modified.

• Revise as required. Based upon the information obtained in the fifth step, we can revise any or all of the previous steps—at any time in the process.

Here is the overall planning model:

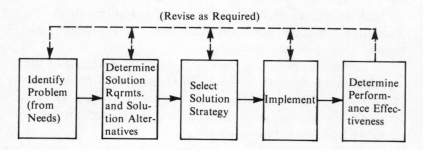

This is a model for intervention, for planned change, for changing the natural order of events. Planning requires change, and change should be efficient and effective. It should also be valid and useful. Unlike the physical sciences, which are primarily designed to observe and describe, this model is intended to change the natural order of things and the natural results; it is a model for interventionists.

Planning is changing on purpose. This planning model calls for a constant interplay between planning and doing. The first two steps are basic to comprehensive planning: determining where we are going, why we are going there (needs assessment, external type), how we will know when we have arrived (objectives and performance requirements), and what alternative ways and means are available for meeting the needs. The last steps of the planning model deal with which of the alternatives to select (picking the processes and inputs that are most useful), managing the changes and interventions (processes), determining performance effectiveness (of products, output, and outcomes), and revising as required.

The generic nature of this planning process. This model is very general—so universal, in fact, that it may be used to solve any problem (if indeed a solution is possible—and if it is not, it will tell you that it is not and what is "missing" for achieving problem resolution). To accomplish any one of the six steps, you simply apply the six-step process for that step alone.

Since the six steps may be used at any level of problem solving, this is a generic process.

Let's take an example. You are assigned the task of evaluating the eleventh grade reading program in terms of learners' gain in reading scores on the Wide World Test of Reading Accomplishment. Since it is your task to determine if the reading program for the eleventh grade is successful, it is assumed that there was an external need identified and justified, that the detailed requirements were identified and alternative ways of meeting the requirements identified, that the best methods and means were selected, and that the program has been implemented—we assume that the first four steps have been accomplished.

We can apply the same six-step planning model to the fifth step alone (in the overall comprehensive planning model)—to determine performance effectiveness. Thus, we can do an internal needs assessment and plan—determine the gaps between the current reading performance and the standardized performance levels for the age. Then we can compare both with the previous levels of performance. (This would be the "product" element in the organizational elements model, figure 2.1, page 42.) So, our first step was to determine gaps to be closed (we know previous performance and standardized test levels; now we are to determine the new required performance). We identify detailed requirements and alternatives (for example, must be completed by June, must be verifiable by the chief of testing, teacher aides might be used to give the tests, it could be made a part of each teacher's job, and so on). Then we go to the third generic step: selecting the solution strategies from among alternatives.

Next we implement the selected methods and procedures (step four) and then move on to the fifth step, determining the performance—identifying and documenting the gaps and drawing conclusions. Finally, we recommend changes and implement them based upon the data and the needs. This starting point assumes that the first four steps have been done and done correctly!

Here is an example with a product type of situation:

You have been requested to determine the value of a program in your halfway house dealing with the improvement of self-concept. In this program, counselors and residents eat breakfast and lunch together and set aside a formal time each day to set new goals and review progress toward existing ones. Together, the counselor and individual residents are to determine where they want to go in terms of personal and learning growth, how well they are progressing, what should be changed, and what should be continued. This program has been going on for seven months. The assistant director now wants to see how well it works, and if it is working well, apply for a grant to continue it.

Given this situation, the six steps could be applied. It is a "product" type of starting place since it seeks to determine the gaps between the achievement of objectives for self-concept improvement and the actual improvement accomplished. Let's apply the planning steps to this problem:

1. *Identify problem from needs.* We have the requirement to determine the gaps between the goal of the program and the accomplishment of that goal. In this case the goal was to help residents grow, which is neither precise nor directly related to an outcome.

2. *Determine solution requirements and identify solution alternatives.* Several requirements exist for this evaluation, such as the requirement that the results must be reliable, must be representative of the phenomenon investigated (in other words, they must actually measure self-concept), must be completed within one month, and must be understandable to the assistant director and perhaps to a state funding agency. Alternative methods and means for this might include applying the Wide-Eyes Self-Concept Inventory, the Purpose-in-Self Test, the National Scale of Personal Orientation, or the Draw-a-Woman Test. The advantages of each assessment vehicle as well as the disadvantages of each are listed.

3. *Select solution strategies from among alternatives.* From the list, the best alternative assessment vehicles and procedures are selected by choosing those which will meet the objectives and will do so with the greatest effectiveness and efficiency. In addition, an experimental design that would yield the desired results is selected.

4. *Implement*. Now the methods and means are selected along with the methods and procedures (experimental design) for gathering the data, and they are put into action. The instruments are obtained, scheduled, and data are collected according to the evaluation plan.

5. *Determine performance effectiveness*. The collected data are reduced and analyzed, and the results are used to determine the extent to which the goals and objectives were accomplished. The discrepancies are noted, and the corrective action possibilities are identified, discussed and considered.

6. *Revise as required*. Based upon the shortfall (gaps that were larger than allowed) and recommended changes, the modifications that are approved are then implemented, and the procedures of the project are modified.*

WHAT DO YOU DO WITH THE NEEDS?

Part of the first generic planning step requires the identification of needs. The resulting selected needs become the "problem" and serve as the validated objectives for further planning, implementation, and evaluation.

With the needs selected for action, you and your organization can be better assured that:
- the problems being addressed are real and important problems,
- the objectives are valid,
- the objectives are in measurable performance terms,
- there is a firm and realistic basis for planning, doing, and evaluating.

The best assurance of utility of goals and objectives comes from doing an external assessment.

---

*Note that the six steps of the planning process were applied for this example. Any time there is a problem to be resolved, the six steps may be applied.

The beginnings of all interventions—programs, projects, activities—rest upon the correctness, appropriateness, validity, and utility of the goals and objectives. Needs assessment is your best assurance of getting the right goals and objectives.

SETTING GOALS AND OBJECTIVES

Goals are intended results that are measurable on a nominal or ordinal scale; objectives are intended results measurable on an interval or ratio scale. Both are important and useful, and both are used to point toward desired results.

Goals and objectives may be set for any result, be they internal or external. Products, outputs, and outcomes may be stated as either goals or objectives—but the more often you can state a result as an objective the better, since objectives are more reliable statements of results, and being more precise and reliable allows us to accomplish more effective, efficient, and rigorous planning and evaluation.

Here are some goals:
- Increase resident participation.
- Make counselors happy.
- Provide learning experiences for future life application.
- Make trainees self-sufficient.

Note that each of these is measurable on a nominal (naming) or ordinal (greater than, less than, or equal to something else) scale. Note that each sets a direction and identifies a purpose.

Following are some objectives:
- Nurses will increase significantly their mastery of patient-practitioner communication as measured by the Growth Corporation materials.
- By June 1, 1986, at least 90 percent of all training specialists will have been certified as competent in Evaluation and Needs Assessment by the State De-

partment of Education Bureau of Special Certification.

- At least 95 percent of all learners in the second grade at Hollie School will demonstrate mastery of all learning objectives specified in the performance guide.

These qualify as objectives because they are measurable on an interval or ratio scale.

Here are some statements of results. Classify them as either goals or objectives:

RESULT	GOAL	OBJECTIVE
Develop an appreciation for music.		
Increase mastery of 90% of trainees.		
All counselors will complete correctly all items within 40 minutes.		
All children will weigh at least 90 pounds before entering the event.		

Do we agree? The first two examples are goals; the rest are objectives.

Here are some steps you might go through to set a useful statement of results. First, set your goals:

1. Identify what it is you want to accomplish.

2. State what should be observable when you have finished.

3. Make certain that your statement of results tells what is to be demonstrated, who or what will demonstrate it, under what conditions the results will be observed, and that the results will be measurable on a nominal or ordinal scale.

Now, state your objectives:

1. Make certain that all of the elements for a goal (above) are met.

2. State the observable results so that you can measure them on an interval or ratio scale.

The difference between a goal and objective lies in the precision of measurement. Both are intentions of desired results.

Both goals and objectives are more useful when they speak to results, not means or processes.

If you are not certain that you have identified a means or a result, just ask yourself this question: "If this were accomplished, what would result?" Keep asking this question until your statement of the goal (or objective) *is* the result.

WHERE TO GO

A needs assessment is designed to tell you where we are, where we should be going, and why. If it is the external variety, it will tell you where you are going, where you are now, and just why, from the point of view of self-sufficiency, you want to get there. Since the external variety deals with gaps in results, we can use the "what should be" part of a need statement as our intended result. Let's see:

What is: At least 73 percent of all learners exiting from the Big Swamp School District during the last five years are self-sufficient as measured by their income being equal to or greater than their outgo as indicated by their being extended credit by at least one major credit card company as certified by a credit check accomplished by the superintendent or her designee.

What should be: At least 95 percent of all learners exiting from the Big Swamp School District during the five years starting at the beginning of school one year from now will be self-sufficient as measured by their income being equal to or greater than their outgo as indicated by their being extended credit by at least one major credit card company as certified by a credit check accomplished by the superintendent or her designee.

This hypothetical example shows a gap between the current results of 73 percent achieving self-sufficiency and the desired level of at least 95 percent achieving self-sufficiency.

Because a result is a statement of intended ends, the "what should be" portion of a needs statement *is* a statement of results. It is thus:

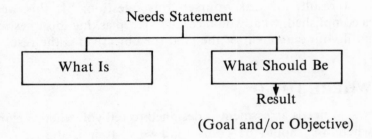

Needs Statement

What Is   What Should Be

Result

(Goal and/or Objective)

Setting goals, then, relies upon determining where you are now, where you want to be at some future point, and stating the intended results in as reliable a manner as possible, ideally on a scale using interval or ratio measures.

The precision of a results statement may be achieved by making sure that it has the following elements and characteristics:

1. *It states what results are to be obtained.*
2. *It tells who or what will display these results (a learner, a teacher, an entire district, a state, and so on).*
3. *It notes under what conditions the results will be observed (in a classroom, on a written test, on the job).*
4. *It specifies what criteria will be used to determine if the results have or have not been achieved. (If we want to make this an objective, it will be measurable on an*

interval or ratio scale. If it is to be a goal, it will be measurable on a nominal or ordinal scale.)

5. *It communicates the intent and the performance standards so that there will be no confusion about what is expected among doers, recipients, and evaluators.*

There are a number of useful presentations on objectives (1, 2, 3, above). All emphasize the requirement for rigor and precision. Some workers differ on whether or not the actual criteria (4, above) should be included in the objective or in a separate statement of criterion measures (4, 5). We recommend that when you are doing overall program planning and evaluation that the statement of objectives include the criteria as part of the objective statement, as we noted earlier. In order to learn to write useful objectives, we suggest you read one of the books on setting objectives. Remember, however, that you want to write a statement that is an objective—measurable on an interval or ratio scale.

ARE OBJECTIVES ALWAYS BETTER THAN GOALS?

We would be less than candid if we did not tell you that the data on whether or not one should use objectives are less than unanimous. An exhaustive review of the literature on the use of objectives showed that while the data are not totally supportive of using objectives, it is clear that their use usually results in better achievement, and it almost never makes things worse. Thus, while the data are equivocal on objectives always achieving better results, we vote strongly for their use.

Drafting statements of intended results is an important matter and should not be approached in a cavalier fashion. If we do not have valid, reliable, and useful statements of intended results, our efforts and evaluation will be wanting. We must care enough to be precise, rigorous, and correct.

It is a simple matter of knowing what it is that is to be accomplished. The greater the precision, the fewer will be the possible misunderstandings. Which of these two statements is least confusing?

- Increase learning in math.
- By June of next year, at least half of the learners who did not pass the functional capability test on math and math applications will have scored at or above the pass level as specified in the test booklet.

The second leaves little doubt about what "increased learning" really means, and further, it tells how one can determine if a minimum desired level of "increased learning" has or has not been achieved.

KEY POINTS

- Planning is done when you want to change what will otherwise happen—on purpose.
- There are six steps in a useful planning process:
    1. Identify problem from needs.
    2. Determine solution requirements and identify solution alternatives.
    3. Select solution strategies from among alternatives.
    4. Implement selected methods and means.
    5. Determine performance effectiveness.
    6. Revise as required. (This revision goes on during all other steps.)
- The six-step model is generic; it may be used any time one wants to plan, and one may start planning at any one of the six steps.
- There are many names for results: goals, objectives, products, outputs, outcomes, ends, "what should be."
- Goals are measurable on a nominal or ordinal scale of measurement; objectives are measurable on an interval or ratio scale of measurement.
- Products, outputs, and outcomes are all results. Products and outputs relate to internal or organizational results; outcomes are external results.

- The "what should be" portion of a needs statement is an objective if it is properly formed.
- There are five characteristics of a usable objective. It states

    What results are to be obtained,

    Who or what will display these results,

    Under what conditions the results will be observed,

    What criteria will be used to determine if the results have been achieved, and

    All criteria and standards so there will be no confusion between recipients, implementors, and evaluators.
- Measurable objectives are not always more effective than goals or purposes, but they are recommended for all purposive planning, doing, and evaluation.

Selected References

1. Mager, R. F. *Preparing Instructional Objectives*, 2nd ed. Belmont, Calif.: Fearon, 1975.
2. Popham, W. J. *Selecting Appropriate Educational Objectives*. Los Angeles: Vimcet Associates, 1967.
3. Kibler, R. J., Barker, L. L., and Miles, D. T. *Behavioral Objectives and Instruction*. Boston: Allyn & Bacon, 1970.
4. Gagne, R. M., and Briggs, L. J. *Principles of Instructional Design*, 2nd ed. New York: Holt, Rinehart & Winston, 1979.
5. Kibler, R. J., and Bassett, R. E. "Writing Performance Objectives." In *Instructional Design*, edited by L. J. Briggs. Englewood Cliffs, N.J.: Educational Technology Publications, 1977.
6. Simon, H. *The Science of the Artificial*. Cambridge, Mass.: Massachusetts Institute of Technology Press, 1969.
7. Kaufman, R. *Identifying and Solving Problems: A System Approach*. 2nd ed. La Jolla, Calif.: University Associates Publishers, 1979.

8. Kaufman, R. "A Possible Taxonomy of Needs Assessments." *Educational Technology* XVII (November 1977): 60-64.
9. Kaufman, R. "Needs Assessment: Internal and External." *Journal of Instructional Development* I (Fall 1977): 5-8.
10. Witkin, B. R. "Needs Assessment Kits, Models, and Tools." *Educational Technology* XVII (November 1977): 5-18.
11. Kaufman, R., and English, F. W. *Needs Assessment: Concept and Application.* Englewood Cliffs, N.J.: Educational Technology Publications, 1979.
12. Reusch, J. *Knowledge in Action: Communication, Social Operations and Management.* New York: Aronson, 1975.
13. Kaufman, R. *Educational System Planning.* Englewood Cliffs, N.J.: Prentice-Hall, 1972.
14. Flanders, N. A. *Analyzing Teacher Behavior.* Reading, Mass.: Addison-Wesley, 1970.
15. Provus, M. *Discrepancy Evaluation.* Berkeley, Calif.: McCutchan, 1972.
16. Scriven, M. *The Methodology of Evaluation.* AERA Monograph Series on Curriculum Evaluation. Chicago: Rand McNally, 1967.
17. Scriven, M., and Roth, J. "Needs Assessment: Concept and Practice." *New Directions for Program Evaluation* I (Spring 1978).
18. Kaufman, R., and Carron, A. S. "Utility and Self-Sufficiency in the Selection of Educational Alternatives." Occasional Paper No. 8. Tallahassee: Center for Needs Assessment and Planning, Learning Systems Institute, Florida State University, January 1979.

5
THE ROLE OF EVALUATION

Let's now relate evaluation to the previous steps. We conduct a needs assessment to tell us the gaps between where we are and want to be. The "want to be" is the goal-setting and objectives-setting part of our total process. The planning steps tell us exactly how to get from here to those goals and do so economically. Evaluation is to determine the extent to which we reached the goals set forth as a result of the needs assessment; and can also tell us whether we are in fact following the steps laid out in our plan. We can tie it to the processes we have described in the following figure.

A clear understanding of that which can (and should be) evaluated, the "gestalt" of evaluation means and ends can be summed up as shown on page 94.

SO?

If we are going to evaluate, we should clearly understand what we are looking at, understand what it is by itself, and further understand how it fits into the whole picture. We can spend much time and effort looking at and commenting upon small slivers and pieces of a total phenomenon (such as a school), but the great power of evaluation is knowing how well each means is working in terms of itself and how it is allowing the total system to operate, or preventing it from operating the way it could and should.

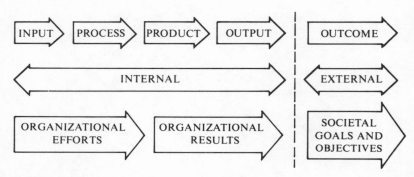

Fig. 5.1

This is not to say that evaluation of parts of a total system is not important. Evaluation is the determination of the value and worth of something. We can look at the value of an effort—for instance, a program of summer youth employment—and determine if the objectives have or have not been met. This determination reveals only the extent to which the planned results were obtained. It says nothing about the value of the experience in assisting the youths to become more self-sufficient, to be happier, to have a better self-concept, or to be more competent. This experience might contribute to these, but it is a moot question unless it investigates those relationships.

Evaluation is multilevel. It can tell the effects of an intervention; it can measure the extent to which change has occurred; and it can speak to the value of the intervention. We propose that all levels are important and useful. We further suggest that the more an evaluation considers the utility of an intervention as seen in a "big picture" of the individual both inside and outside an institution or program, the more useful will be the information obtained. When the "big picture" is reviewed, and interventions are seen in a context of individual self-sufficiency and performance, then more useful decisions about interventions may be made. Sooner or later someone has to put all of the organizational "pieces" together. Often it is the learner or client as she copes in society. It would be most useful if the educators, trainers, counselors, the society, and the learners/clients shared in the planning and evaluation. With such sharing of intentions and results, then—together—better decisions will be made.

AN EXAMPLE

You are a teacher of reading in a public school, job training center, or college or industrial remedial program. You have been asked to evaluate the reading materials sent by the Growth Corporation and report back to the reading consultant and your associate teachers.

What do you do?

First some questions:

1. What is reading?

2. Evaluate what?

3. Why evaluate?

4. What is it I want to see happen as a result of the evaluation?

5. Does the program make a contribution to "larger ends"?

Let's deal with these in terms of this "means-ends" model. What is reading? It is a means: it is the ability to encode and decode symbols on the part of learners, and to do it to some reference standard. Evaluate what? The intention seems to be to determine the extent to which the reading materials bring about predictable changes in the learners' skills, knowledges, and attitudes about learning—to allow-them to perform at a specified, useful level. It further requires that a determination of reading skill elements be identified and measured.

Why evaluate? So that we can determine if the reading materials under study do what they say they are doing, and further (although usually never stated exactly) see if they teach skills, knowledges, and attitudes which are worth mastering.

What is it we want to see happen as a result of the evaluation? We want to see materials which allow learners, when they legally exit the educational or other agency to be able to be self-sufficient, contribute and be happy in the world outside—in society. This aspect, too, is not often stated, but merely implied.

Let's look at this practical situation in terms of our organizational elements "matrix"—our figure on page 72.

The Inputs are:

- Teachers with state certification or similar qualifications, including skills, knowledges, and attitudes toward learners and learning.
- Learners with entry skills, knowledges, and attitudes.
- The Growth Corporation materials, including their objectives, materials, and procedures.
- The school's or program's resources and facilities, and the rules, regulations, and policies of the school (and/or district), project, city, state and federal governments.
- The money or funds (or time) to conduct this evaluation.
- The techniques available to implement the materials, including team teaching, differentiated staffing, open-plan curriculum.
- The supervision and management supplied by the teachers, teacher aides, and administrators.
- The curriculum of which these reading materials are a part.

- The anticipated skills, knowledge, and attitudes of the learners using the materials.

The Processes include:

- The Growth Corporation materials, including the instructions and the ways and means to implement them.
- All how-to-do-its which are involved with the use of the Growth Corporation materials, including the actual application of human and physical resources.

The Products include:

- Mastery of the objectives of the Growth Corporation materials, in whole or in specified learning segments.

The Outputs are:

- The learners who exit from the educational agency or program with degrees, diplomas, or certificates of completion.

The Outcomes include:

- The learners who get jobs after leaving school.
- The ability of the graduates to be self-sufficient and contribute to society—now and for the next twenty years or more.

Any useful evaluation of this hypothetical situation would take into consideration the following elements:

- What are the inputs into the Growth Reading Materials usage?
- How well did the procedures, materials, and activities involved in the Growth Corporation Materials—the process work?
- What do they produce (in terms of learners' skills, knowledges, and attitudes) and how do these "products" square with the "advertised" objectives of the materials?
- Do these "products" contribute to the outputs—do they contribute to meeting graduation requirements; and
- Do the graduates of the programs equipped with

these reading skills, knowledges, and attitudes become self-sufficient and contribute better than without the use of these materials?

Actually, these last two questions are difficult to measure precisely, but any good evaluator will know that they are important questions, and some inferences will be useful. If we decide to do only part of this total "evaluation" then we should limit our discussion and know what we are not covering.

For instance, if we only looked to determine if the objectives of these materials were met, and never traced the progress of the students completing the materials through the balance of school and/or out into the society, we might never know if the materials were useful to the learner in the larger society outside of school or the program. The learning materials (or any tool or intervention) are best understood as part of a larger system—one intending to help learners complete useful education (output) and then become self-sufficient outside (outcome).

An evaluation should keep in sharp focus the boundaries of its activities, findings, and recommendations. If the evaluation is for a narrow focus alone (effectiveness of a reading program, impact of praise as a motivator, and so on), then this should be clearly known before starting the evaluation and faithfully reported with the results. If, however, the evaluation is broad in nature and intention, if it intends to look at both effects, the context of the effects, and the impact upon the whole person as he or she works and lives in society, this too should be a part of the evaluation planning and reporting.

The scope and role of evaluation should be clearly understood by the evaluator and the persons reviewing the evaluation results. Without specifics about what was intended and the level of generality, inferences are bound to be made which might not hold water.

The key concept here is that evaluation is relative to the

parts and the whole of a system. We can do all of it (a "good" evaluation) or part of it (a practical or expedient evaluation), but we should firmly understand what we are doing and what we are excluding.

Don't fool yourself or others. A report of an evaluation effort might well list the objectives and results categorized and summarized in terms of the organizational elements—inputs, processes, products, outputs, and outcomes. All are important and related.

APPLICATIONS IN EVALUATION

Following are some examples from various intervention frames of reference. We are going to mix up the examples in terms of the disciplines and specialties, for the ideas we are presenting here are usable in any intervention context. We want to get you thinking about asking useful questions and knowing how to get the right answers.

Here are some examples for a program or activity that will emphasize each of the following:

Input
Process
Product
Output
Outcome

In this section we will set the stage and determine what evaluation questions should be asked. In Chapter 6, based upon these same examples, we will show you evaluation techniques to deal with each element and each set of questions.

JOB RETRAINING—INPUTS

The city of Gotham has decided to do something about its unemployment rate. Last year it was 9 percent; this year it is hovering at 10.5 percent. The mayor has set up a special commission to study the problem, make recommendations to him and the council about the jobless, and make some recommendations on what to do about the situation. They have studied the problem and their report is ready to be delivered. How can we tell if the report is useful or not?

This is basically a two-element study. It looks at inputs and processes: who is unemployed and what should be done to decrease unemployment. The characteristics of the unemployed (or underemployed), the nature of the jobs for which they might be trained and qualified, and the resources available to them are all inputs. Possible methods and techniques for helping the unemployed are processes.

Some of the questions which might be asked here are:

What is *unemployment?*

What is *underemployment?*

Who is unemployed or underemployed?

What are the characteristics of these unemployed or underemployed persons (age, sex, educational background, language skills, and so on)?

What jobs might be filled by them in the future?

What are the laws governing such people? What programs are available to them?

What resources are being used now to help these people?

What resources might be made available in the future to help these people?

What are the requirements for making these people employable? Successful?

All of these questions focus on inputs. What about the other part of the report, the part concerned with ways of helping? As soon as you hear the word *help,* you can immediately think of *process.* Questions to be answered here might include:

What kinds of programs have been used in other states and cities to help similar people?

Does this situation have some requirements that demand new or modified programs and methods?

Can on-the-job training be used?

Can we get these people jobs that pay enough to cover the cost of training?

What methods, techniques, vehicles, and plans will meet all or most of the objectives?

In this example, the processes must be fitted to the inputs if the intervention is to be a success.

Of added importance are questions of *product* (What are the job-entry components for the various jobs these persons can be trained for?); *output* (What are the certification/licensing, total job-entry requirements for completion and ability to be hired?); and *outcome* (What are the requirements for economic and personal self-sufficiency in Gotham for the duration of this program?). The emphasis is on organizational efforts, the inputs and processes, but organizational results and outcomes should also be considered.

THE NURSES' TRAINING PROGRAM—PROCESS

Saint Theresa Hospital had one of the best nurses' training programs in the Midwest. It was a three-year program, one of the few left in the country. While many other programs trained physicians' "handmaidens," this one had a reputation for training and placing nurses who got jobs and went on to supervisory positions. The graduates were trained well, and they were confident.

The new dean of nursing had attended a seminar at a national training conference on mediated instruction and competency-based instruction. She was impressed, and thought she saw a way to improve the effectiveness and efficiency of her program.

She called her staff together and shared with them her new insights and experience. It was a close-knit team already, and they decided, with only two dissenters, to try building some self-instructional modules into the anatomy and respiration segments of the program. In addition, it was decided to try competency-based instruction and testing, and a select group went about identifying competencies so that the exact behaviors desired would be identified, serve as the basis for instruction, and finally form the basis for evaluation.

The competencies were developed, tried out on a group to check for consistency and completeness, and passed with flying colors. The self-instructional modules were developed and formatively and summatively evaluated (tried out along the way and revised as required, and then tried out on a group typical of the population for which they were intended). They, too, were found to be successful.

It was decided to shift the curriculum in this direction as soon as possible and to seek a grant from the government for the subsequent work.

The hospital director and the guidelines for the proposal both required evaluation. The staff thought they had done enough, but an evaluation consultant stated that while they had used good techniques, they were incomplete.

Here the emphasis is upon *process*. Some of the questions to be answered include:

How well do the self-instructional modules meet their objectives?

Do the materials relate well to the required content?

Are there any more efficient and effective ways to promote learning?

Is it worth the cost of development in terms of what it delivers?

Should all content be taught using the same self-paced techniques?

Are the competencies actually correct?

While these are the main focus of attention—process— there are some additional questions that could be asked, questions of input, product, and output, as well as outcome. Let's look at some of these related issues:

Input: What are the characteristics and requirements of the learners in the program?

Is the staff competent to develop the media and the competency statements?

How much money is available for this work?

Product: What was learned?

Was the learning that took place with the new approaches more efficient or effective than what took place after using other methods?

Were performances on the part of the student nurses equivalent to or better than their performances using other or previous methods?

Output: Would this method improve the rate of graduates?

Would this training allow more graduate nurses to be licensed or to get better jobs?

Outcome: Do these methods make the graduates more competent on the job as indicated by improved patient health, fewer accidents, and so forth?

Even when the focus is on process (how-to-do-its), other organizational elements are of importance.

DRUG COUNSELING—OUTPUTS

California is where the "good life" is. Many people go there to live, to work, and some come to try to get a new start in life.

Some who come have emotional problems, and some get into drugs. Some of these get arrested, become depressed, and when they do, sometimes there is a requirement not for punishment, but for help.

A small central valley town had its fill of "hopheads." The city council heard a presentation dealing with drugs and reformation of addicts, and wanted to help. They noted that even some of the children of solid citizens in town had become addicted. Blame and name-calling did no good, and they wanted to get the youngsters off drugs.

They had heard about a drug-oriented agency in Los Angeles in which the clients lived in and took part in therapy games, and they heard about other approaches as well.

They did not have much money, but they wanted something that worked, and they wanted it *now*.

They hired a consultant from the local university who was experienced in humanistic psychotherapy, clinical psychology, and drugs treatment. The consultant had run a small clinic herself and had produced some good results. She was charged with coming up with a plan, getting the plan approved, and getting the center operating and successful. It was a challenge, and she accepted it.

She hired some assistants, and they did an audit of programs in the state and looked at data from each. They looked at successes and failures, looked at the characteristics of the drug abusers they worked with, and noted the relationships between methods and results for each type of individual. Some programs worked better with minorities, others with highly educated people, and so on.

A report was prepared that showed various methods studied and recommended an approach. It had a budget, projected results, a timetable, and a staff.

It took two sessions in the town council, but it was approved as proposed, and the counseling center was initiated.

The research was instituted, and while treatment was going on, intake and results data were accumulated.

Reports were filed on the number of clients seen, entry characteristics of the clients, number of sessions, and progress of clients. The center was busy, and most were satisfied with what was happening.

The counselors had weekly "rap sessions" where they compared notes and commented on tough cases, made suggestions to each other, and subjectively reviewed cases for possible discharge. At one of the meetings, a new councilperson asked for an evaluation of the center. He wanted to know what was happening and whether it was worth continuing, halting, or expanding.

The evaluation here will have an emphasis on product and output. Here are some of the product questions:

PRODUCT

How well are the counseling techniques working?

Are all counselors getting the same results?

Is this better than comparable methods used in other centers?

Are clients satisfied with their progress?

Are clients moving along from stage to stage of counseling in a satisfactory manner?

Here are some output questions:

OUTPUT

How many are getting discharged as completed?

Are all types of clients being discharged equally, or are there some differences?

In addition to these evaluation questions, some more should be attended to:

OUTCOME

After discharge, do clients stay off drugs for more than a year?

After discharge, are clients able to be self-sufficient, to get and keep jobs, and to maintain family and person relationships?

On the following page is a "sorting" of the elements in this drug counseling example into the categories of the organizational elements.

Fig. 5.2 is a hypothetical example of the "what-should-be" portion of the organizational elements model, for the drug counseling "case."

KEY POINTS

* Evaluation can apply to the end results of a program or the ways in which it is implemented.
* An important role of evaluation is to help determine outcomes—the effects of a program on an individual's long-term functioning in society.

	INPUTS	PROCESSES	PRODUCTS	OUTPUTS	OUTCOMES
What is	1)	2)	3)	4)	5)
What should be	6) Who are the counselees? Who are the counselors? What resources do we have?	7) Are the counselors working the way they should? Are resources available when they should be? Are there differences in various therapy and treatment activities? Are the methods all working the same, or are some better than others?	8) Are the counselees building the skills and attitudes necessary for discharge? Is therapy successful? Are all counselors getting the same results?	9) What is the discharge rate? Are all types of clients being discharged equally?	10) After discharge, are clients off drugs for more than a year? After discharge are all clients self-sufficient, self-reliant, off welfare? How many discharges are coming back or are getting arrested?

Fig. 5.2

- Survival and self-sufficiency are the ultimate goals of any intervention.
- There are brief descriptions and key questions asked about the following types of programs:
  - a job retraining center
  - a nurses' training program
  - a drug counseling program
- A matrix shows how to tie evaluation to the organizational elements in a hypothetical example.
- An evaluation can be conducted for any one or group of organizational elements.

Selected References

Kerlinger, F. N. *Foundations of Behavioral Research.* 2nd ed. New York: Holt, Rinehart & Winston, 1973.

Provus, M. *Discrepancy Evaluation.* Berkeley, Calif.: McCutchan, 1972.

Scriven, M. *The Methodology of Evaluation.* AERA Monograph Series on Curriculum Evaluation. Chicago: Rand McNally, 1967.

6
TYPES OF EVALUATIONS

Evaluation models come in many varieties and are useful in different contexts and environments. In Chapter 4 we saw that there were two basic types of needs assessments: external and internal. Each type is designed to answer different questions.

Evaluation models are also designed to address different questions and to begin at different points. Although the usual emphasis of the various models is on the internal workings of the programs, the results of those workings (the product) could also be used with the external needs identified; or those relating to outcomes. The various models can be used with either internal or external needs and are simply guides or frameworks; you as the evaluator fill them in with the needs you and your colleagues have identified.

The ultimate goal of all the models is to support and assist in useful decision making (not to make the decisions for you). The quality of the information available for the decision-making process is directly related to the meaningfulness and validity of the needs, goals, and objectives you've identified. Thus, before selecting and implementing any of the evaluation models, be sure that the groundwork is adequate.

As we mentioned earlier, it is best if the statements of intended results are objectives and can be measured with interval or ratio level data. The quality of the evaluation is dependent upon the quality and accuracy of the measurement.

You must limit the number of questions you want to answer or you will be overwhelmed with data. It is better to start small and do a good job, especially the first time.

TYPES OF EVALUATIONS

How do you know when you're there? That is, how do you know that your program is successful (other than by intuition or other nonscientific, seat-of-the-pants methods)? Earlier, we talked about needs assessment and discussed how to use a needs assessment to help you determine where you should be headed.

Once the gaps have been defined and quantified, the next step is the selection of an evaluation design. (The term *design* here refers to the conditions and procedures used by evaluators to collect data.) There are several designs or models of evaluation, each having a slightly different purpose and useful in slightly different situations. There are two reasons for including the various models: 1) to provide you with a variety of options for your own evaluation efforts, and 2) to take some of the mystery out of the jargon and cryptic terms and letters used by some professional evaluators. The models we've selected to include are:

- Scriven's Formative-Summative Model
- CIPP Model
- CSE-UCLA Model
- Stake's Countenance Model
- Tyler's Goal Attainment Model
- Provus's Discrepancy Model

- Scriven's Goal-free Model
- Stake's Responsive Model

Don't be overwhelmed by this list. We've chosen to include a variety of models so that you can see the diversity of approaches to the evaluation of programs and program outcomes. Some of the models are useful both during and after the program (Scriven's Formative-Summative, CIPP, Stake's Reponsive Model), and some are particularly useful in decision making (CSE-UCLA, Provus's Discrepancy model). Thus the "menu" is varied and the selections presented here are by no means exhaustive of the ways of conceptualizing the manner in which program evaluation can take place. But the more aware you are of the possible courses of action you have available in dealing with the identified gaps, the more likely you are to make the best use of available data. Also, when people are aware of and understand the options and alternatives available to them, they are likely to make a better decision.

SCRIVEN'S FORMATIVE-SUMMATIVE MODEL

Scriven's conception of evaluation involves a set of extrinsic criteria (or the outputs) and pays attention to the quality of the goals. Scriven suggests that evaluation is more than determining the extent to which goals have been met; it is also an assessment of the extrinsic worth of the goals themselves.

If the goals are not worth achieving in the first place, why then is it of interest to determine if these goals have been met? We've emphasized that evaluation is humane and should help improve matters. However, if particular program goals are judged to be inhumane, it is within the duties of the evaluation team to make recommendations as to what appropriate goals might be.

Formative evaluation involves the assessment of progress toward the identified goals while the program is still in progress. Under this model, "midstream measurements" would be taken, and the extent to which the program appeared to be meeting these criteria could be assessed. If the program seems to be progressing well, fine. However, if a particular method—such as an instructional strategy, or the use of media—is not working as intended, this intermediate feedback could be used by the program designers to make the necessary changes before more time and money are spent. A formative evaluation is concerned with questions such as these:

- Does the program seem to be working as originally planned?
- Are all components of the program functioning effectively, or do some of them require revision?
- Based upon the progress data, should the program be implemented elsewhere?
- Are there serendipitous events that should be incorporated into the formal structure of the program?

Thus, formative evaluation is especially useful to program designers. It can give them feedback before the entire instructional package is delivered so that modifications and adjustments can be made. In this way, the program developers have the option of increasing the effectiveness of the program through changes designed to tailor the program or instruction to the identified needs of the client group.

Summative evaluation, on the other hand, is useful in determining the extent to which the final, end-of-project goals of the program were actually met. It is an after-the-fact event, at a time when recommendations for program changes may well be influenced by the availability of time, money, and staff to implement the program a second time.

Summative evaluation addresses questions such as these:
- What do the clients know about the content that was taught?

- To what extent have attitudes and/or behaviors been changed as a result of this program?
- Have the goals and objectives set forth by the program developers been met?

When implementing the summative evaluation model, care must be taken to measure the actual effects or results of the program rather than some extraneous influences that might have influenced the students. For example, if an achievement test indicated that the desired level of knowledge was not attained, was it because the test did not reflect the content of the instruction, or was it because the instruction was delivered in a way that made it unnecessarily complex and incomprehensible? Care must be taken to select and/or design appropriate and valid instruments. In addition, special attention should be paid to these questions.

- Did the program truly make a difference?
- Did the program meet and fulfill the identified needs and objectives?
- Were the gaps identified in the needs assessment filled?
- Are the students performing at the level specified in the goals statements?

As an example of the formative-summative evaluation model, let us look at the development and pilot testing of one component of the Women's Re-entry Program, "Interview and Job Placement Skills." The stated goal of this component is to provide the skills and information necessary for clients to compete successfully in the interview situation. The goal did seem to be of value, since it would help contribute to the self-sufficiency of the clients.

The program consists of a series of two-hour classes which meet three times a week for six weeks. During the sessions, participants learn tips on grooming, manners, makeup, and the appropriate attire for various situations. Another portion of the program deals with the actual behavior in the interview situation—practice answering questions, as well as asking questions about the job. The third component of the program is field practice—interviews with personnel officers on site.

The formative evaluation would take place during the six weeks the program was in operation, and would address questions of particular interest to those who had designed the instructional materials and activities. During the first two weeks, emphasis is placed on grooming, makeup, and appearance. If the instruction is meaningful to the clients, they should begin to change their outward appearance, and dress for class as if they were preparing for a job interview. Observations on the part of the instructor can provide data here. If no changes are apparent, why is this? How should the instruction be changed to make it more relevant to the participants?

Other data useful for the formative evaluation include attendance records, informal comments from the participants, and scores on any tests that may be given. A note of caution: don't get participants overinvolved in critiquing the program. They may become overly critical and not master the content of the course.

Summative evaluation takes place after the completion of the program, and addresses issues such as the overall effectiveness of the program. Examples of data useful for the summative component would be end-of-course ratings of the participants by the personnel officers and successful experience in obtaining job interviews at the end of the course. The end-of-program question to be addressed is: Are the clients performing at the level indicated in the objective? The answer would be "yes," "somewhat," or "no." If it is either of the latter two, recommendations should be made for program changes so that revisions in program content and/or delivery can be made.

CIPP MODEL

The emphasis in the CIPP model of Stufflebeam and Guba is on the provision of information for decision makers other than the evaluator. In his Formative-Summative model, Scriven emphasized the necessity for determining the worth of the goals and the provision of information for program designers and implementors. In the CIPP model, the emphasis is exactly the opposite. Data are collected and information presented to someone else who will determine its worth.

An important element is identifying, obtaining, and providing information which will be used in the process of developing decision alternatives. The identification of information is usually done jointly, with the evaluator and decision-maker each assuming an active role in specifying the type of information required. Then, the actual data collection and analysis is performed by the evaluator. The third step is the provision of information as a basis for decision making, and again is a cooperative effort between the evaluator and decision-maker.

In this model, the evaluator is often a person not directly connected with the program, but one who works with those involved in the program (the decision-makers, or those who are ultimately responsible for the "go/no go" decision). Note that the evaluator works with the program staff in specifying the information to be collected as well as in providing insights into the provision and interpretation of data used in the decision. Thus, the CIPP model requires team effort with emphasis on cooperation among those planning, as well as carrying out the evaluation.

To assure that important evaluation elements were included in evaluation, this model identifies them with the first letter of each dimension as part of its name: *C* is the *context*; *I*, the *input*; *P*, the *process*; and the other *P*, *product*. (It should be noted that these labels are different from those used in this book. Later in this chapter we will help you translate between this model and ours.)

The essence of this model is seen in the definition of evaluation given by Stufflebeam, one of the designers of the model: "Evaluation is the process of delineating, obtaining, and providing useful information for judging decision alternatives."

Each segment of that definition provides an action statement for the evaluator and defines the three basic steps in this model:

Delineating refers to the type of information required by those making the decisions. The specification of the information and data is accomplished by means of a dialogue between the evaluator and the decision maker. Jointly they discuss and define the data that are necessary and arrive at a plan for obtaining the data. The specification process would include the formulation of goals and objectives and the identification of the data that would provide the information.

Obtaining refers to the actual data collection process. The evaluator is in charge of collecting the data as planned in the delineating process. The data analysis would also take place in this phase. The emphasis here is upon the collection and preparation of the information required for the decision-making process. The burden of the evaluator can be reduced at this point through the active cooperation and participation of people identified in the resource inventory.* Some data may already be available, and teachers or others may be willing to assist in the data collection process.

Providing refers to the rendering of the information in a manner that increases its usefulness to the decision maker. This would include the synthesis of the information and the preparation of tables and charts that will help the work of the decision maker. Preliminary interpretations of the data could be made by the evaluator. However, as in the delineating stage, the evaluator should work closely with the decision

---

*The resource inventory is the list of tools, instruments, people, and other resources available to you to use in the evaluation process.

maker. The statements made on the basis of the evaluation should represent a collaborative effort.

Note that the emphasis in all three phases (delineating, obtaining, and providing) is on information, information for decisions. What types of decisions are possible with the CIPP model? Stufflebeam has identified four types of decisions that are possible, based on the CIPP model. Each of these types of decisions has a corresponding type of evaluation (and it's from these types of evaluation that the model gets its name):

Decision	*Evaluation*
1. Planning (to determine objectives)	1. Context
2. Structuring (to design instruction)	2. *Input*
3. Implementing (to use or improve instruction)	3. *Process*
4. Recycling (to judge products, outputs, or outcomes)	4. *Product*

Usually all four segments of the CIPP model are used, as the process of decision making can be used throughout the planning, designing, implementation, and assessment of an instructional technique. Each is useful in particular settings or aspects of a total program. However, one may choose any one of the four phases if this best meets the requirements of the evaluation.

Context evaluation is useful in the earliest phase of program development: the identification of needs and the designing of a rationale for the program. Typically, a thorough description of the existing program is developed, and then the present is compared with possible or potential programs, or the "should be." Through this process a specific set of objectives is developed. These objectives are then used to design an instructional program.

Input evaluation is useful in identifying what actually will be required to meet the objectives defined in the context evaluation. Can existing resources be reallocated, or will additional resources be necessary? Again, the emphasis is on the gathering of information to be used by decision makers. Here the decisions revolve around the issue of how to structure the instructional program to make the best use of resources in obtaining the identified program objectives.

Process evaluation has many things in common with formative evaluation. Both are used while the program is being delivered and are useful in determining if the program is being delivered as it was originally planned. The in-process, or ongoing, evaluation is particularly useful in identifying strengths and weaknesses of the program that might not be identified after the conclusion of the program. An example would be an observation of the instruction and teacher-student interaction while teaching was taking place. Data gathered here can be used to improve the program before it is too late. This aspect of the CIPP model differs from Scriven's formative evaluation in that the emphasis here is on the gathering of information to provide a basis for informed decision making about the progress of the program rather than making the actual program change.

Product evaluation occurs during as well as after the program, with the emphasis on the gathering of the information necessary for decisions to be made regarding the program. As noted earlier, a "recycling" decision can be made. Should the program be continued, modified, or terminated? Should the objectives be redefined? What are the appropriate decisions to be made regarding the disposition of the program? Again, the emphasis is on provision of the data necessary to make an informed decision.

As you can see from the description of the CIPP model, it is quite comprehensive and is useful during all phases of program design, development, and implementation. It is more comprehensive than Scriven's Formative-Summative evaluation model in that it provides data for decision making during the planning phases as well as the implementation and end-of-program assessment. Because it is concerned with program development from the very beginning, this evaluation model could begin with an external needs assessment—or at a look at the outcomes—and incorporate these identified needs into the program planning. However, the CIPP model, like the other models discussed here, is usually used for internal efforts and thus usually only deals with what we call process, products, and outputs.

The CIPP model is particularly useful when a relatively thorough documentation of needs, objectives, and goals is required, and would be a good choice when designing a proposal for a program to be submitted to a funding agency. For example, one piece of information often required by funding agents is the development of a rationale for the identified objectives of the proposed program. The process of context evaluation would help in this aspect of planning in that the status of existing programs is described, and then the programs are evaluated to the extent that they address the problems or gaps. This complete documentation of the existing programs, and the fact that they do not adequately meet the identified needs, should provide a sounder basis for program development.

The input evaluation would be useful in proposal development in that it could provide information on the allocation of necessary resources for the proposed program. The identification of existing resources useful for the delivery of the program could help the program developer formulate a more realistic estimate of the costs and resources required to implement the program. A full description of the available resources would also permit more informed choices as to the best methods of allocating resources to meet particular program objectives.

The process and product evaluations obviously could not be completed during the proposal writing process. However, they can provide guidelines for the information to be gathered both during and after the delivery of the program. The evaluator should be a part of the entire program planning process under the CIPP model.

CSE-UCLA MODEL

The CSE-UCLA model gets its name from the location at which it was developed: the Center for the Study of Evaluation at the University of California at Los Angeles. Like the CIPP model, this model emphasizes the provision of the information required by decision makers. As you read through the description of the CSE model, you will note many similarities between it and the CIPP model. Both are quite comprehensive and are useful throughout the entire planning-development-assessment process.

Like the CIPP model, the CSE model requires that a series of decisions be made at each of several stages:

Stage 1. To what extent are the instructional programs meeting the objectives for which they were designed? Is there a discrepancy between the current status of the program and the desired status? This identified discrepancy may be termed a *need* and can be used to identify goals and objectives. The decision to be made during this first stage is: What exactly is the problem? Is it defined narrowly enough so that a set of objectives can be formulated and a program designed to meet these objectives?

Stage 2. What types of instructional programs will meet the needs identified in Stage 1? Are there commercially developed programs that are suitable? The emphasis here is on the planning of a program to meet the needs identified in Stage 1. The decision here concerns program selection, or the decision that a program must be adapted or developed.

Stage 3. Is the program being carried out as was specified in the original plan? Many times changes are made during the delivery of the program. These changes should be identified, described, and evaluated in terms of the degree to which they facilitate the attaining of the objectives. The focus of Stage 3 is the issue of the validity of the implementation of the program. The decision to be made is based on the identification and modification of changes in the program, and entails decisions concerning further changes that would keep the program on course in terms of attaining the specified objective.

Stage 4. To what extent is the program meeting the objectives? Special attention is given to products that have been developed during the program up to this point. Are there some components of the program that are more successful than others? What products are available from these successful components? The decisions of Stage 4 are similar to those of Stage 3: the requirements for program modification. The difference between the two stages is the emphasis on the products in Stage 4 rather than on the processes as in Stage 3.

Stage 5. What is the overall worth of the program? To what extent did it meet the identified objectives? The decisions to be made here are: What will happen to the program? Will it be implemented, revised, or dumped? Value judgments of the overall worth of the program may also be made here, based on the conclusions and inferences made from the data collected.

The CSE model is useful in many of the same situations as the CIPP model. The stages of the two models are very similar with the exception of the process stage (CIPP) which has been reconceptualized into two stages in the CSE model (Stage 3—implementation, and Stage 4—program improvement). Thus, this evaluation model would also be a good choice in designing a proposal for submission to a funding agent.

Another use of these models would be in the development of a monitoring system to ensure that appropriate and meaningful questions are asked during the entire program-

development process. Since we used the proposal development example for the CIPP model, we will consider the
development of a monitoring system here.

The use of the CSE model in monitoring the design,
implementation, and overall success of the program should
provide better quality information and documentation concerning the impact of the program. It seems too often to be
the case that questions are asked only in stages 3, 4, and 5,
and assumptions about the soundness of the rationale for
the objectives and program design are made intuitively.

During Stage 1, the emphasis is on the gathering of
descriptive information about the community, the mental
health facility, the clients, as well as society as a whole. In
monitoring this aspect of the program, particular attention
should be given to the identification of the problem, the
needs, and the gaps. No list of problems or needs should be
taken at face value. Rather, questions concerning the relationship between the identified needs and the ultimate happiness and self-sufficiency of the client group at the mental
health facility should be addressed. Needs, goals, and objectives should be based on information (data)—not on a
general consensus of "this is good, or should be done."
Thus, in monitoring this aspect of the evaluation, one should
seek information, data, and documentation of the identified
needs.

Stage 2 monitoring involves raising questions about
why particular program alternatives were selected. A consideration of the potential impact of the various programs
available would take place here. For example, several already
existing programs may be identified as possibly useful in
fulfilling the identified objectives. Each set of materials
should be carefully assessed to determine the extent to which
it meets the identified objectives, or the extent to which it is
"exportable" (useful in another, different setting). Research
data from other institutions would be useful during this
stage. In monitoring Stage 2 evaluation, one should never

accept a particular program selection for implementation unless there is evidence (data) concerning the potential impact of the various program alternatives, and evidence that this particular program represents the best "fit" for the needs, goals, and objectives identified during Stage 1. Too little data or too few questions at this point may yield less than optimum effectiveness of the overall program. As we mentioned earlier, too often Stage 1 and Stage 2 data are considered "givens"—and are not adequately documented (or questioned).

Stage 3 involves the actual implementation of the program. During this stage, the monitor should be carefully attuned to what is going on—whether the program is being implemented as it was intended. Observations of the program, the clients, the instructors, and the setting, can provide valuable insights as to what is happening. On site information can be useful to help determine whether the program is being delivered exactly as specified.

Stage 4 involves program improvement, and would incorporate the information gathered in Stage 3. Monitoring at this stage would involve the identification of those components of the program that seem to be working as intended, and those that do not seem to be working. The monitor questions why particular components work and others do not, and attempts to shed light on the overall dynamics of the program.

Stage 5 involves the overall, end-of-program statement of the effectiveness or worth of the program. The monitor may help determine the extent to which the identified objectives were fulfilled, but could also look for other data relating to the overall quality of the program. Sometimes a Stage 5

There is a variety of materials designed for practitioners wishing to use the CSE-UCLA model, probably more so than for any of the other models, which are available from the Center for the Study of Evaluation at the University of California, Los Angeles, CA 90024.

evaluation involves comparing pretest and posttest scores on tests. Evidence such as the attitudes, perceptions, or feelings of the participants may not always be considered, yet would seem to be an appropriate area of questioning and concern in documenting the worth of a program.

STAKE'S COUNTENANCE MODEL

The two preceding models of evaluation, CIPP and CSE-UCLA, emphasized the *decisions* to be made during the evaluation. Stake's model adds another dimension: description. He terms the decision-making process *judgment.* Stake's model is similar to the CIPP and CSE in that all three are intended to be comprehensive and begin the evaluation process during the planning phase of program development.

Stake identified three aspects of an educational program and suggested that an evaluator be concerned with factors that may impinge on the programs during each of these three phases. The first is the *antecedent phase,* or the period before the program is implemented. What events are taking place? Will these events in any way affect the results of the program? The description of the antecedent phase would also include the identification of *conditions* existing prior to the program that might affect the result.

The second phase is *transaction,* or the actual process of instruction. What exactly is happening during the delivery of the program? Is the program being delivered as was intended by the program developer? The third phase is *outcome** or measures of the effect of the program after its completion. Did the program do what it was supposed to do? Are the clients performing at a higher level than they were before the program?

*Note that this would be the same as our use of the word *product* or *output.* This use is relating to an internal result.

Within each of the phases, Stake proposed two types of descriptions and two aspects of judgment. With the descriptive portion of his model, he distinguished between intents (what the planners intended to occur) and observations (what actually took place). Thus, for the antecedent phase, the evaluator would describe the intended preconditions as well as the actual preconditions. (This would in reality be an identification of gaps.) During the transaction phase, the intended instruction would be described, as well as the instruction that was actually delivered. (Again, the emphasis is on the identification of gaps.) Likewise, the outcome phase would be composed of a description of the *intended* outcomes (results) as well as the *actual* outcomes (results).

The decision-making or judgment aspect is divided into two separate concerns: standards and the actual behavior of making the judgment. Standards refer to *how* the judgment will take place. Will the worth of the program be judged by comparing it with another program? Or will the program be compared with a set of absolute standards not directly related to the program? Again, as with the description portion of the model, the activities of determining the standards and making the actual judgment take place during all three phases: antecedent, transaction, and outcome.

A distinctive feature of Stake's model is that it forces the evaluator to describe the events, activities, and conditions that exist before, during, and after the implementation of the program. This careful and thorough description will provide a wealth of information about both the intentions of the program developers and on-site observations of what actually occurred during each of the three phases.

Another distinctive feature of Stake's model is the specification of the standards that will be used in making the decisions or judgments. Although both the CIPP and CSE models emphasize the decision-making process, neither model forces the evaluator or the client to specify the standards against which the program is judged. Therefore, it appears that the use of the Stake model provides for: 1) more descriptive information throughout all phases of the evaluation, and 2) the explication of the standards to be used. Because of the concern for the specification of the standards to be used in the judgment, the use of independent judges is possible. That is, given a set of data, and a set of standards, persons not directly connected with the program should be able to determine the merits of the program.

SUMMARY OF ACTIVITIES
WITHIN THE COUNTENANCE MODEL

Antecedent Phase:
(period of time before the program is implemented)
DESCRIPTION
- Intents (what goals are specified, what effects are desired)
- Observations (data concerning the activities and events taking place during this phase; description of existing conditions)

JUDGMENTS
- Standards (criteria to be used as basis of comparison)
- Judgments (the process of comparing the intents, observations, and standards)

Transactional Phase:
(period of time during which the program is implemented)
DESCRIPTION
- Intents (the planned instructional intervention)
- Observations (actual daily behavior of clients and instructors, including the use of media, tests, and so forth in delivering the program)

JUDGMENTS
- Standards (criteria to be used as the basis of comparison)
- Judgments (the process of comparing the intents, observations and standards)

Outcome Phase:
(the period of time immediately following the delivery of the program during which most of the "outcome" data are collected)
DESCRIPTION
- Intents (What are the intended or predicted outcomes of the program?)
- Observations (the data gathered at the end of the program; often test scores, course grades, and similar measures of achievement)

JUDGMENTS
- Standards (criteria to be used as the basis of comparison)
- Judgments (the process of comparing the intents, observations, and standards)

TYLER'S GOAL ATTAINMENT MODEL

Tyler's Goal Attainment model of evaluation is one of the earliest of those described here. The emphasis of this model, as implied by its title, is on the determination of the extent to which the goals defined for the program have been attained. The important first step in the use of this model is specification of the goals. A distinctive feature of this model is the devising of goals in terms of the student, society, and subject matter. Each goal (and there can be numerous goals) is transcribed into a behavioral objective that is measurable. The concern with measurable results of the program is incorporated into the earliest planning phases, something that is not a part of the other models discussed, even with their emphasis on the provision of information for decision making. After the program has been delivered, the measurements, as specified in the behavioral objectives, are gathered, and the success of the programs is judged in terms of the extent to which the goals have been attained. Thus, the thrust of the goal attainment model is the evaluation of the results of the instruction, or the extent to which the goals, stated in terms of behavioral objectives, were achieved.

Tyler's model is less comprehensive than several of those described here, but it has one very important aspect not explicitly stated in the other models: the statement of the goals in terms of measurable behavioral objectives. Since results must be measured before the decisions can be made, the concern with measurement early in the planning stages is very important.

PROVUS'S DISCREPANCY MODEL

The *discrepancy* in the title of Provus's model is the discrepancy between the standards set for the basis of judgment and the actual performance of the students during and after the completion of the program. Thus, as with Stake's model, the standards to be used in the judgment of the success of the program must be stated at the outset. However, the decision to be made about the success of the program involves more than the comparison between the actual performance and the standards, for, if a discrepancy is found, a decision must be made as to whether to change the program or the standards. (Other models of evaluation do not mention the possibility of changing the standards—just revising the program.)

The use of the discrepancies between the predetermined standards and the actual performance is not a one-shot activity as with the Tyler model. After a thorough documentation of the intention and objectives of the program and a specification of the standards to be used, the discrepancy evaluation begins. There are four times during the installation, delivery, and completion of the program that the discrepancy analysis is done.

The first is during the installation phase and involves questions such as this: Is the program being installed as the designers intended? If discrepancies are noted, a decision must be made as to whether to proceed anyway, to change the installation, or to terminate the program. The second discrepancy analysis comes during the actual implementation phase and addresses issues similar to those suggested by Scriven's formative evaluation. This question is asked: Does the program seem to be working as it was intended to work? Discrepancies noted here may precipitate decisions to alter, continue, or dump the program, depending upon the magnitude of the discrepancies noted. The third discrepancy analysis occurs after the program has been completed and addresses questions such as this: Did the program fulfill the objectives for which it was designed? Discrepancies noted here can be used to judge the worth of the program in terms of the objectives that were specified initially.

The fourth discrepancy analysis goes beyond the other models discussed in that it is concerned with a cost-benefit analysis of the program as compared to the cost-benefits of other programs.

Although Provus's use of discrepancies at the various stages of program implementation differs from the emphasis of the CIPP and CSE models, all three emphasize the provision of information for decision making. Provus's model does include one additional piece of information—the cost-benefit analysis. With this one exception, all three models are very similar.

The above models, although in some respects quite diverse, have one thing in common: they provide information about how well the program, or various components of it, are meeting the objectives or goals for which they were designed. Thus, they are goal-based; they consider only those results/products that are specified in the statements of the objectives and goals of the program.

SCRIVEN'S GOAL-FREE EVALUATION

It has been suggested that paying attention to the pre-specified goals limits the amount (and sometimes the quality) of the information available for decisions about the program. By expanding one's view to the totality of the program rather than only that specified in the goals statements, one may document the intended as well as the unintended results.

Scriven proposed goal-free evaluation in an attempt to provide a broader base of information for the evaluation process. In those evaluation models in which the products, or outputs, of the program are compared with the goals set for the program, any serendipitous results or side effects would not be included in the main evaluation process and might be overlooked altogether. The emphasis then is on *results*—whether they were planned or unplanned. The premise of goal-free evaluation is that by not limiting oneself to, or biasing the evaluation with the stated goals, the evaluator can be more open to the total impact—positive and negative, intended and unintended—of the program.

One of the challenges—as well as advantages—of goal-free evaluation is that one must be able to specify the variety of ways in which a program could have potential impact on the clients, and then collect appropriate information (test scores, observations, informal interviews) to determine the actual impact. In fact, the only means of identifying serendipitous results is with goal-free evaluation.

When evaluators confine themselves to looking only at prespecified goals, or the intended effects, they may get tunnel vision and miss some very important results of the program. When an evaluation looks at the goals, or intended results of the program, some of the actual results may be ignored or overlooked, and the task of determining the importance and quality of the results may be made more difficult, or perhaps even impossible.

Goal-free evaluation does not have to be free of *all* goals, but it must be free of the *producer* or *program* goals. Societal goals, consumer goals, or even the goals of the funding agency might be considered, but note that these may or may not be directly connected with the program.

However, if evaluators do use any of these goals, they will have to show that the goals are in fact appropriate to the present evaluation. Evaluators cannot arbitrarily assign goals to a program and then evaluate it on that basis. In goal-free evaluation, the evaluators identify what has occurred—both positive and negative—and report all these results. The overall judgments about the impact of the program are made based on all of the data, not just on that which reflects the planned goals.

Let's say a goal-based evaluation was planned as an integral part of the program development progress. (All of the above evaluation models are goal-based; that is, they relate results to goals.) Further, suppose that base-line data were collected that reflected only the goals of the program as they were clearly stated at the outset. But what if, during the implementation of the program, it became apparent that the program wasn't working quite right and required some changes—and a modification of the goals? What about the base-line or pretest data collected before the program began? These may or may not be what are required to measure the changes, results, or impact of the program. An instance such as this is one where goal-free evaluation could provide more information than a goal-based evaluation.

However, there are many other reasons for considering goal-free evaluation. It can be used to identify other worthwhile things that have happened as a result of the program—things perhaps not thought about as the program and the goal-based evaluation were planned. For example, does community acceptance of the program seem very positive? Is there a growing number of persons wanting to enroll in the program? These are the kinds of data that could be collected to document the effectiveness of the program in addition to those data collected for the goal-based evaluation.

Goal-free evaluation can also be used after the program has been delivered, much as summative evaluation. Here the evaluator would examine the materials, perhaps interview the teachers, and collect a variety of data reflecting what he or she perceived to be possible results of the program. By not knowing the program goals, the evaluator is freer to consider a wider range of results, some of which may not have been inferred from or even obscured by the program goals.

Goal-free evaluation should not lead one to abandon goals completely. Goals are desirable and necessary for program planning and design as well as for implementing the program. However, in the evaluation process, goals may lead evaluators to overlook some side effects of the program, simply because they weren't expecting them, weren't looking for them, and did not collect any data to document them.

USING GOAL-FREE EVALUATION

Goal-free evaluation can be used during the program (formative evaluation) or after the program (summative evaluation). It can be internally or externally based. In other words, it is useful in a variety of settings and may be used during or after the program by those involved in the program delivery process or by those outside the program.

Let's look at how it could work at the end of the program.

First, the evaluators (*not* the program developers) examine the materials from the program to determine the content, format, mode of presentation, reading level, and other factors.

Second, they plan data collections around these observations and results. Note that since the evaluators are not limited in their thinking and planning in designing the data collection to the goal of the program, they are more likely to identify those data that will provide a more complete picture of the actual impact of the program.

Third, based on the data collected reflecting program goals as well as other unanticipated, unplanned outcomes, the evaluators summarize the impact of the program.

During the course of the examination of the materials,

they may infer some of the goals of the program. However, these inferences should not preclude the examination of all possible results of the program, both intended and unintended.

A goal-free evaluation may be used in conjunction with any of the goal-based models discussed above. By using both approaches the amount of gap filling (meeting identified goals) and the side effects, both positive and negative, may be identified. Using both models would address such questions as: To what extent were the goals identified actually met, and in so doing, were there any negative effects on the client group? Such a situation could arise if a program met its goal of raising the reading level one grade level, but had an unexpected side effect of a tremendous increase in the outside work of the teacher. This probably would be considered a negative effect.

However, goal-free evaluation could also be used to identify positive, unintended outcomes. Suppose the goal of a job training program was the successful placement of 75 percent of the graduates. This would be an intended goal. However, suppose it was observed that the attitudes of employers of the graduates were overwhelmingly positive— an unplanned, but certainly a very positive outcome. A goal-based evaluation would probably miss this important piece of information, yet a goal-free evaluation was able to detect this unintended result.

STAKE'S RESPONSIVE EVALUATION MODEL

Several years after Stake designed his "Countenance" model, he proposed another, less "hard data oriented" model which he called "responsive evaluation." (Hard data refers to test scores or other types of number data.) An important difference between the responsive evaluation model and his earlier model is the decreased emphasis on the precision of measurement, the collection of pretest and posttest data, complex statistical analyses, and an increased concern with the usefulness of the findings for persons involved in or interested in the program.

The style and method of communicating the results of the evaluation also differ. In the responsive model the emphasis is on natural communication of the results rather than the preparation of a formal evaluation report. The type of evaluation report usually prepared for other methods of evaluation provides information about what happened as a a result of the program, but usually very little about what the program was actually like. We may be able to specify what gaps were filled, but may not be able to describe the specific activities used to fill the gaps. Thus, we have information about what, but not about how. The other types of evaluation models discussed above are concerned with specifying the objectives or intents of various programs, and then, through the various data collected, providing information about how well the objectives were met. The responsive model, on the other hand, is directly concerned with the program activities; with describing what is happening.

The responsive evaluation model is particularly useful in evaluating arts and humanities programs and other similar type of programs where specifying aims, purposes, and accomplishments is extremely challenging. In addition, explicit statements of intent are usually not necessary to determine the value or worth of these types of programs. However, the responsive evaluation model should not be used as an alternative to specifying objectives and documenting gaps when these activities are of primary concern.

Figure 6.1 (on page 134), shows the prominent events in a responsive evaluation. The evaluation process may begin at any "time" on the clock.

Now that we've discussed some of the distinctive characteristics of the responsive evaluation model, let's look at how to do one. First, the evaluation plan must include an emphasis on observing the program activities. Throughout

Talk
with clients,
program staff,
audiences

Assemble
formal
reports,
if any

Identify
program
scope

Winnow,
format
for audience
use

Overview
program
activities

Validate,
confirm,
attempt
to disconfirm

Discover
purposes,
concerns

Thematize;
prepare
portrayals,
case studies

Conceptualize
issues,
problems

Observe
designated
antecedents,
transactions
and outcomes

Identify
"data needs,"
re, issues

Select
observers,
judges,
instruments,
if any

Figure 6.1 Prominent events in a responsive evaluation. (Used with permission of the author.)

the entire evaluation process, the tasks of observation and feedback are critical. The audience, the program staff, and other persons in the community can do observations in addition to the evaluator. Care must be taken to include a variety of viewpoints so that both positive and negative feedback are possible. Observations from a variety of sources are combined to give a broad view of the program and its activities—from several points of view, representing diverse values.

Unlike the types of evaluations discussed above which proceed along in a specified manner, the steps or tasks within responsive evaluation may occur in a variety of orders; some steps may be repeated, while others may be omitted. A usual beginning point is talking with clients, program staff, and audiences about the program scope, activities, and issues. Several times during the evaluation these same people may be contacted to provide feedback to the evaluator, or perhaps to supply additional information. Other tasks include obtaining any available reports or other printed information, identifying program scope, surveying program activities, identifying purposes of the program and/or concerns relating to the program, conceptualizing issues and programs, and identifying data "needs," in particular, those relating to the issues. Often data consist of observations which form the basis of case studies. The case studies, or other means of portraying the information, may be shared with the program staff and/or audiences to verify the accuracy of the observations and perceptions. This dialogue and interaction are the responsiveness. The dialogue and feedback are particularly important when evaluating the arts and humanities because in any artistic endeavor there are different values for different persons. Thus, the evaluator is very much a participant rather than an outside observer. He or she works with people to a much greater extent than in any other evaluation model. The validity of observations are checked out with the program staff as well as with the clients or audiences. Interaction, dialogue, and responsiveness are evident throughout the entire evaluation process.

When is responsive evaluation useful? As with goal-free evaluation, it can be used in conjunction with goal-based models. It is useful during formative evaluations in describing the ongoing activities, and in "troubleshooting" when no one is sure what might go wrong. It is helpful in summative evaluation in providing an understanding of the program activities, with their strengths and weaknesses.

Responsive evaluation is not appropriate if you are primarily concerned with documenting whether certain goals have been met. Since hard data (test scores) are seldom collected, results of responsive evaluation are not expected to be as reliable and objective. However, a responsive evaluation does provide valuable information to decision makers in the form of describing and documenting the activities of the program so information is available to describe what happened *during* the program, as well as the final results.

RELATING ALL THE EVALUATION MODELS

Figure 6.2 summarizes these evaluation models and indicates where in the evaluation process, from input to outcome, the various models are useful. In some cases, the usefulness of a particular model is intended when goals are written, for example, in terms of outputs or outcomes, rather than being limited to just products. Thus, for the goal-based models, some of their usefulness may be limited artificially by the limitations of the goals formulated by the program designers, who do not fully realize the relationships among the three types of results: products, outputs, and outcomes.

Figure 6.2. The relationships between the organizational elements model for evaluation, and those others which are representative of useful models in the field. The variables of each of the extant models are compared with the organizational elements. Note that for these other models, the terms "product," "output," and "outcome" are used almost interchangeably and thus run the risk of only dealing with internal results. (See opposite page.)

	INTERNAL			EXTERNAL	
Model	Input	Process	Product	Output	Outcomes
Formative Summative		Formative	Summative (depending on scope of program and goals)		
CIPP	Context, input	Process	Product		
CSE	Stage 1	Stage 2	Stage 3	Stage 4	Stage 5
Stake	Antecedent	Transaction	Outcome		
Tyler	Goal Identification	Attainment	(depending upon the goals)		
Provus	Installation	Implementation	Fulfill Objectives? (depending upon objectives)	Cost ———— Benefit	
Scriven's Goal-Free					
Stake's Responsive Model					

SELECTING AN EVALUATION MODEL

At this point, you may be asking yourself, "Why did I get involved in all this?" So we'll remind you of the usual reason for doing an evaluation—to answer questions and make decisions. As you saw from the variety of evaluation models, there are many options to choose from, and that's part of your responsibility as an evaluator—to specify exactly what questions you want answered.

The needs assessment discussed earlier in the book will provide a framework for *what* questions to ask. However, it is up to those involved in the evaluation process to determine the focus of the evaluation. It is up to the program designers, program managers, and all other partners in the evaluation to specify the exact focus.

- Are you interested in finding out the extent to which the program fulfilled the specified objectives?
- Are you interested in comparing your program with a standard?
- Do you want to see if the program is working the way it was intended to work?

We may choose to evaluate any one of the organizational elements. The scope of the evaluation should hinge on your decision, relative to what questions you want answered.

It's not possible to solve all of the world's problems with one evaluation or one research project. Thus, when we decide on the focus of our evaluation, we are really specifying the questions we want to answer. If we try to answer every possible question relating to all phases of the planning-implementation-product-output-outcome phases of the program, we are literally trying to address all possible questions anyone would ever want to ask about the program. However, in trying to please everyone, we will probably end up pleasing no one. By trying to specify—and answer—all possible questions rather than focusing our efforts on something that really interests us (and may well make a difference in our program), we are emphasizing quantity rather than quality.

The worth of an evaluation is seen in the quality and usefulness of both questions and answers. Whenever the focus is too broad and we haven't specified the questions narrowly enough, we may become too overwhelmed by the quantity of information (data) we have to gather to address all the questions, and the quality of the entire evaluation effort may well be lessened.

Therefore, you must decide exactly what it is you want to know. Several of the evaluation models provide for a very comprehensive approach to the assessment of your educational program. But what if, for example, you are interested in determining whether your program seems to be working as planned and you like the ideas of the discrepancy model? Fine. Go ahead and use that portion. If you decide you want to answer questions about the actual *process* of instruction and that's all, go ahead and use a "piece" of a model. If you decide in the beginning what is the most important part of the identified problem to be addressed and then concentrate on doing a good job, you probably will succeed.

Use the information in Figure 6.2 to help you decide which pieces of which models to use. You must be able to specify where in the organizational elements continuum you want to evaluate, or where decisions should be made.

1. *Where on the continuum do you want to begin?*
2. *Where on the continuum do you want to end?*
3. *Are you concerned with the extent to which goals are fulfilled? (If you are, use one of the goal-based models.)*
4. *Are you concerned about identifying* all *of the results of the program? (If you are, use goal-free evaluation.)*
   NOTE: *You may use goal-free evaluation in conjunction with any of the goal-based models.*

Now you are ready to select the model, or pieces of the models, to use. Figure 6.2 on page 137 will help you select those portions of the models relating to where you want to ask questions and make decisions.

In order to make sure you have as complete an evaluation model as you require, place each of the objectives (or questions you have to ask) in the educational elements matrix:

INPUTS: Were there enough trained teachers to do the job?

PROCESSES: Did the Growth Corporation materials do what they were supposed to do? Were they administered correctly?

PRODUCTS: Was there a significant increase in reading mastery as measured by pre–post-test comparisons?

OUTPUTS: Did this intervention increase the number of learners graduating?

OUTCOMES: Did the graduates who took part in this procedure get and keep jobs more successfully than those who did not participate?

If you have most or all of the questions only in input, processes, and products categories, you might have some problems generalizing your findings to other schools or agencies. Most people restrict evaluation research to the first three organizational elements, but you might want to expand these usual horizons.

The most important part of the whole evaluation process is the ability to make statements and conclusions that address the gaps identified in the needs assessment. If particular parts of the evaluation models serve your requirements, use them. Don't feel that you must adopt a model in its entirety if the results of the implementation of that model will not be useful to you and the other team members who are making decisions about the programs you're involved in.

Although some of these evaluation models emphasize the supplying of data to decision makers, our opinion is that the evaluation is not complete until the decision has been made and the *value* of the whole procedure determined. It is important to have useful information concerning program, projects, and action. It is useful, however, only when there is a decision to continue, modify, or stop a program or activity. If the evaluation information is not used, then it has been useless, or futile. If a decision is made not to change anything, then it should be based on evaluation information. The point here is that we strongly advocate that evaluation *include* the supplying of information to decision makers, and that it also include the decisions themselves and the results of the decisions in the form of recommendations for action and the resulting impact from carrying out decisions.

KEY POINTS

- Evaluation models provide a variety of options and formats for conducting the evaluation.
- The eight models included are some of the more commonly used models, but by no means exhaustive of the possibilities.
- Evaluation models are useful in helping provide data for decision making; but part of evaluation also involves making decisions to continue, stop, or modify.
- The results of evaluation are only as good as the data (goals, objectives) that go into the evaluation.
- Results of measurements do not make decisions; they do provide data for decision makers. Evaluation uses measures to make decisions.
- Limit the number of questions you want to answer with the results of the evaluation.
- Quality questions generaly provide a greater opportunity for quality answers.

Selected References

1. Scriven, M. "The Methodology of Evaluation." In B. R. Worthen and J. R. Sanders, *Educational Evaluation: Theory and Practice*. Worthington, Ohio: C. A. Jones, 1973.
2. Bloom, B. S., Hastings, J. T., and Madaus, G. F. *Handbook on Formative and Summative Evaluation of Student Learning*. New York: McGraw-Hill, 1971.
3. Scriven, M. "Evaluation Perspectives and Procedures." In J. Popham, *Evaluation in Education: Current Applications*. Berkeley, Calif.: McCutchan, 1974.
4. Stufflebeam, D. L. *Evaluation As Enlightenment for Decision Making*. Washington, D.C.: Association for Supervision and Curriculum Development, 1968.
5. Stufflebeam, D. L., et al. *Educational Evaluation and Decision Making*. Itasca, Ill.: F. E. Peacock, 1971.
6. Stufflebeam, D. L. "Alternative Approaches to Educational Evaluation." In J. Popham, *Evaluation in Education: Current Applications*. Berkeley, Calif.: McCutchan, 1974.
7. Stufflebeam, D. L. "A Depth Study of the Evaluation Requirement." *Theory into Practice* 5 (1966): 121–133.
8. Alkin, M. C. "Evaluation Theory Development." *Evaluation Comment* 2 (1969): 2–7.
9. Worthen, B. R., and Sanders, J. R. *Educational Evaluation: Theory and Practice*. Worthington, Ohio: C. A. Jones, 1973.
10. Popham, W. J. *Educational Evaluation*. Englewood Cliffs, N.J.: Prentice Hall, 1975.
11. Klein, S. P., et al. *Evaluation Workshop: An Orientation. Leader's Manual and Participant's Notebook*. UCLA-CSE. Monterey, Calif.: CTB, McGraw-Hill, 1971.
12. Amor, J. P., and Dyer, J. S. *A Decision Model for Evaluating Potential Change in Instructional Programs*. Los Angeles, CA. UCLA-CSE, 1970.

13. Stake, R. E. "The Countenance of Educational Evaluation." *Teachers College Record* 68 (1967): 523—540.

14. Stake, R. E. "Objectives, Priorities, and Other Judgment Data." *Review of Educational Research* 40 (1970): 181—212.

15. Tyler, R. W. "General Statement on Evaluation." *Journal of Educational Research* 35 (1942): 492—501.

16. Metfessel, N. S., and Michael, W. B. "A Paradigm Involving Multiple Criterion Measures for the Evaluation of the Effectiveness of School Programs." *Educational and Psychological Measurement* 27 (1967): 931—943.

17. Provus, M. *Discrepancy Evaluation.* Berkeley, Calif.: McCutchan, 1971.

18. Provus, M. "Evaluation of Ongoing Programs in the Public School System." In *Educational Evaluation: New Roles, New Means,* edited by R. W. Tyler. 68th Yearbook, National Society for the Study of Education, Part II. Chicago: NSSE, 1969.

19. Provus, M. *Teaching for Relevance: An In-service Training Program.* Chicago: Whitehall, 1969. (Good discussion of use of his model in working with teachers.)

20. Scriven, M. "Pros and Cons about Goal-free Evaluation." *Evaluation Comment* 4 (1972): 3.

21. Salasin, S. "Exploring Goal-free Evaluation: An Interview with Michael Scriven." *Evaluation 2* 1 (1974): 9—16.

22. Scriven, M. "Goal-free Evaluation." In E. R. House, *School Evaluation: The Politics and Process.* Berkeley, Calif.: McCutchan, 1973.

23. Stake, R. *Evaluating the Arts in Education: A Responsive Approach.* Columbus, Ohio: C. E. Merrill, 1975.

24. Wholey, J. S., et al. "Evaluation: When Is It Really Needed?" *Evaluation 2* 2 (1975): 89—94.

25. Stake, Robert E. *Program Evaluation, Particularly Responsive Evaluation.* Paper #5 in Occasional Paper

Series. Western Michigan University, Kalamazoo, 1975.

26. Bateman, Worth. "Assessing program effectiveness: A rating system for identifying relative program success." *Welfare in Review*, 1968, *6* (1), 1–10.

27. Caro, Francis G. "Issues in the evaluation of social programs." *Review of Educational Research*, 1971, *41* (2), 87–114.

28. Dubois, Philip H. and Mayer, E. Douglas. (eds.) *Research strategies for evaluating training*. AERA Monograph Series on Evaluation, No. 4. Chicago: Rand McNally & Co., 1970.

29. Knox, Alan B., Mezirow, Jack, Darkenwald, Gordon G., and Beder, Harold. *An evaluation guide for adult basic education programs*. New York: Center for Adult Education, Teachers College, Columbia University, 1974.

30. Grotelueschen, Arden D., Gooler, Dennis D., Knox, Alan B., Kemmis, Stephen, Dowdy, Irene, and Brophy, Kathleen. *An evaluation planner*. Urbana, Ill.: Office for the Study of Continuing Professional Education, University of Illinois, 1974.

7
TOOLS OF EVALUATION

Statistics are tools and represent a set of techniques designed to help organize data in order to provide useful information for decision making. Note that we didn't say they would make the decision for you; there's a big difference. You are the decision maker.

Statistics are most frequently used in evaluation to *describe* data, events, or clients and to *draw inferences* about changes or relationships observed in the program. Statistics provide the tools to help you make decisions based on the results of your evaluation. It is a wise person who knows which tools to use, and when and why to use them.

There are various statistical techniques that are appropriate for the various scales of measurement we've been talking about in Chapter 1, pages 10 to 15. As we said earlier, interval data are the "best" kind to try to collect for most evaluation studies, because there is a greater variety of statistical techniques that can be used with interval data than with any other type of data.

In the next few pages, we will describe some of the more common statistical techniques for both describing your data and making decisions about results and we will talk about why and where these various techniques might be useful. We will *not* be concerned with the computations. You can check the statistics books in the references for an appropriate formula. Many of these techniques are now available in computer programs; check with a computer center. Rather, our concern here is with helping you to be able to specify *what* you want to know, and then use resources (books and/or consultants) to complete the actual computation.

There are two benefits possible from studying this section. The first, and most obvious, is that you will be able to make a more informed decision about the type of statistical technique that best fits the purposes of your evaluation and will provide answers to the questions you've identified.

Another benefit, perhaps a bit less obvious, is that you will become a better and more informed consumer of research and evaluation reports, and you will understand more of what you read when you look at the results of evaluations done by others. Do their results make sense? It is good to be able to judge for yourself, rather than to depend on the opinions and judgments of someone else.

DESCRIBING YOUR DATA

In this section we will show you how to describe your data with numbers and with pictures. You may decide to use both methods—which is perfectly all right!

Let's suppose you just want to describe what's going on, not make any comparison, just describe. A measure of central tendency will tell you something about the typical performance of the group. If you had to select one number that best represented all the clients (or scores or whatever) in the group, a measure of central tendency would be a good choice. There are three, depending upon the kind of data you have:

Nominal—mode
Ordinal—median
Interval or ratio—mean

(For help in identifying your kind of data, see Decision Map I, page 170.) These measures can help answer questions such as these:

Which model of car is sold most frequently? (model = category or nominal data; mode)

Which mineral represents the medium or "average" amount of hardness? (hardness = ranking or ordinal data; median)

What is the "average" score on the ABC math test? (Score = interval data; mean)

A measure of central tendency, then, provides information about the average element in the group. This one piece of information, by itself, can possibly present an unrealistic picture of what's going on. On some occasions, for example, the median may present a more accurate picture of interval data than the mean. Such an occasion would arise when there are a few scores that are very high or very low, and atypical of the rest of the group.

Often when you use a measure of central tendency, you will also use a measure of variability to indicate whether the scores (or whatever) are quite similar (little variability) or very diverse (much variability). This is especially true for various types of test scores, especially for achievement-type tests. For example, if an achievement test were given before a program began and the results indicated that a great deal of variability existed (scores ranged from very high to very low), it would. be helpful, or at least meaningful, to know whether at the end of the program all students or clients were performing up to a certain standard with little variability. Thus, even though we may know that the average performance (score) increased, it is also good to know that the differences among students or clients have been lessened.

Measures of variability include:

Nominal data—range of number in categories
Ordinal data—quartile deviation
Interval or ratio data—standard deviation

What kind of information does a measure of variability provide?

A measure of variability indicates something about the spread or range of values present in your data. The larger the number you computed as the measure of variability, the greater the spread of values in your data.

Which is better, a large or a small amount of variability?

It depends on your purpose. Neither can be judged "good" or "bad" without more information. Would you, as the program evaluator, consider few individual differences (little variability) to be desirable at the conclusion of a program? If so, then "small is good." So the meaning of the size of the measure of variability is up to the evaluator and depends on the goals specified.

Use of both a measure of central tendency and a measure of variability gives a more complete description of your data—an indication of what the "average" element looked like, as well as how diverse, or how similar, the group is.

PICTORIAL DESCRIPTIONS

Graphs, charts, and diagrams are some of the methods we use to display data pictorially. We use these techniques to help communicate information about the data we've collected, to help the reader visualize our data and perhaps understand it a bit better. The details of how to construct the various graphs, charts, and diagrams can be found in any standard statistical text, along with the computations for the numerical data description techniques. In this section, we will briefly describe some of the more frequently used techniques.

FREQUENCY DISTRIBUTION

The data elements (often test scores) are ordered and then grouped in some logical way, usually to give you 8–10 categories or intervals. The following example uses scores from a measure of self-concept.

Scores	Number of People or Frequency
61–70	3
51–60	7
41–50	15
31–40	6
21–30	2

We have lumped together groups of ten scores; these are sometimes called *intervals*. We can look at the frequency distribution and see that fifteen people scored in the 41–50 interval. Since there are fewer numbers in a frequency distribution than in a list of scores, it is usually easier for the readers to draw conclusions from the data. It is quite easy to scan the above chart and conclude that more people scored in the interval of 41–50 than in any other.

CUMULATIVE DISTRIBUTION

A cumulative distribution, either frequency or percent, is used to convey the information, "50 percent of the sample scored at or below" a certain point. We'll use the data from the frequency distribution as an example for the cumulative distributions.

Scores	Cumulative Frequency	Cumulative Percent
61–70	33	100
51–60	30	91
41–50	23	70
31–40	8	24
21–30	2	6

Based on these distributions (frequency and percent), we can say that twenty-three persons, or 70 percent scored at or below 50 on the measure of self-concept.

The above representations of data on charts did make the data easier to read. But there is an even more readable way to present data—with graphs. There are three basic types of graphs: histograms, frequency polygrams, and cumulative percentage or "ogive" graphs. The graphs are used most often with interval or ratio data. Examples of all of these graphs are given below for a set of test scores. Note that in labeling the charts, all have frequencies (or percentages) up the side and the scores (or whatever the variable) along the bottom. This is a convention that is commonly used, and remembering it will help you interpret other people's data and graphs.

HISTOGRAM

Plot at the lower limits of the intervals (or groups of scores). The width of the bar extends over the entire interval. The assumption is made that the scores or observations are evenly distributed over the entire interval. In our example, we would extend the width of the interval from 21–30, 31–40, and so forth.

FREQUENCY POLYGON:

Plot at the midpoints of the intervals (or groups of scores). The assumption here in plotting is that the data are grouped at the midpoint, or the middle of the interval, and that the middle is the most representative score. For example, the first interval in the example is 21–30. The midpoint of this interval is 25. Thus 25 appears on the baseline of the graph.

Histogram

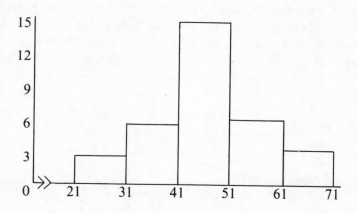

Frequency Polygon

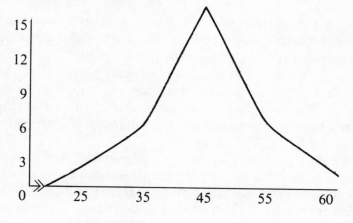

self-concept scores

CUMULATIVE PERCENTAGE, OR "OGIVE"

Using the same data as for the cumulative frequency and percent distribution example on page 150, we can plot either a cumulative frequency or cumulative percent curve. The cumulative percent curve has a special name: *ogive*. To plot an ogive curve, label the side with the percentages, and the baseline with the scores. Using a cumulative frequency distribution (as on page 150), convert to cumulative percentages (as example on p. 150). the percent for each interval, using the top score of each interval for the plotting point. For example, the first interval, 21–30, has 6% of the sample in it, and would be plotted on 30.

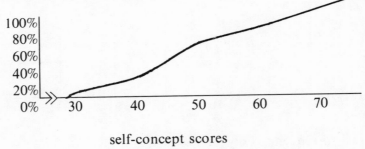

self-concept scores

A cumulative frequency graph can also be constructed similar to the ogive. The only difference is that cumulative frequencies rather than percentages are plotted.

The graphs just described (frequency polygon, etc.) were for data of at least interval measurement. Note that the score intervals were in fact equal appearing, and that the graphs could be interpreted in terms of comparison of scores (higher than, etc.)

Sometimes we may wish to use pictorial representation for nominal data or data that represents categories such as Chevrolet, Ford, and so forth. Bar graphs and pie diagrams are appropriate for this type of data since we want to show differences (or similarities) in membership in various categories.

Pie diagrams are often reported in terms of percentages for the various categories, with the whole of the pie representing 100 percent. Consider the following example of ethnic group membership within a particular sample: In a group of 83 subjects, 41 were Canadians, 23 were Mexican, 15 were Italian, and 4 were Portuguese. The number of subjects in the various ethnic groups conveys some information, but the pie diagram below showing the relative percentages conveys more information at a glance:

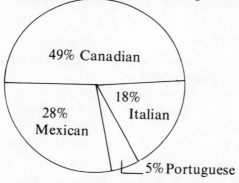

You may often see budgetary information presented in newspaper articles using pie diagrams.

Bar graphs are also used to depict nominal data. Using the same example as above but not transforming the data into percentages, we could draw the bar graph below.

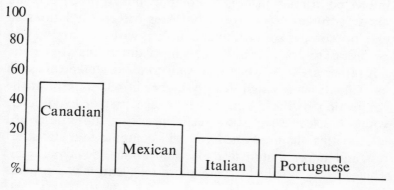

Note that since the data are not in intervals, we don't concern ourselves about plotting at upper or lower limits. We simply place the bars on the baseline with the height of the bar indicating the number of observations in a particular category.

MAKING INFERENCES FROM YOUR DATA

Before you begin to consider which statistical technique you will be using, to help make inferences about your data, you must be able to specify exactly *what* you want to know. Do you want to:

- *know if students performed better (scored higher) after an instructional program?*
- *compare the performance of clients who have completed the program with clients who have not had the instruction?*
- *see if there is a relationship between the performance of the clients and their attitude toward the program?*
- *see if there is a difference in job placement rates between those who have completed the program and those who have not?*

These questions reflect relationships between variables, or comparisons (between groups or scores). If you are interested in relationships or comparisons (differences), you must formulate a pair of hypotheses for each relationship and/or comparison (difference) you wish to study. Hypotheses are not necessary for simply describing your data, but rather are used when you want to make statements such as "Clients scored significantly higher in self-concept at the completion of the program." For each pair of hypotheses, you will select a statistical technique from those described later in this chapter. Then you will compute that statistical test and make a statistical decision about the hypotheses. This process is called *hypothesis testing*, and it is a process that must be completed before you can go on to the important task of formulating conclusions and recommendations for action based on the results of your evaluation. The following sections will help you understand, and be able to use, the process of hypothesis testing as a tool in decision making.

FORMULATING HYPOTHESES

Hypotheses come in pairs and represent a formal statement of the alternatives of the statistical decision: there is a difference or not, or there is a relationship or not. The statement of no difference is called the *null hypothesis*. Thus, a null hypothesis is a formal statement of the research questions in a *null* form. Here are two examples of null hypotheses: "There is no difference in achievement in mathematics after completion of the Math Skills Program as compared to performance before the program" and "There is no relationship between completion of the program and successful job placement."

Since hypotheses come in pairs, we must write an *alternate* hypothesis for each null hypothesis. The above examples, in pairs, would look like this:

Set 1:

Null: There is no difference in achievement in mathematics after completion of the Math Skills Program as compared to performance before the program.

Alternate: There is a difference in achievement in mathematics after completion of the Math Skills Program as compared to performance before the program.

Set 2:

Null: There is no relationship between completion of the program and successful job placement.

Alternate: There is a relationship between completion of the program and successful job placement.

In almost all evaluations you will have several pairs of hypotheses, because you probably will want to make several decisions about various aspects of the program. The place to begin is with the list of questions you want answered and then to formulate pairs of hypotheses for each.

Formulating Hypotheses: Steps

1. Specify the questions you want to answer in the evaluation.
2. Formulate one set of hypotheses for each question you want to answer.

For each set:

a. One hypothesis of the pair is called the "null" hypothesis. It states *either* "There is no relationship . . ." or "There is no difference . . ."

b. The other hypothesis of the pair states exactly the opposite: "There is a relationship . . ." or "There is a difference . . ."

An example:

Questions to be answered:

1. Do clients score higher in self-concept after the program?
2. Do clients with a high self-concept also succeed in job interviews? (Restated: Is there a relationship between self-concept and success in job interviews?)

Set of hypotheses for question 1:

Null: There is no difference in the self-concept scores of clients at the end of the program as compared to their scores before the program.

Alternate: There is a difference in the self-concept scores of clients at the end of the program as compared to their scores before the program.

Set of hypotheses for question 2:

Null: There is no relationship between self-concept and success in job interviews.

Alternate: There is a relationship between self-concept and success in job interviews.

TESTING HYPOTHESES

In this section, we will consider two basic types of hypothesis tests: those concerning relationships and those concerning differences.

DETERMINING RELATIONSHIPS

Do your hypotheses concern relationships? If so, the appropriate test of the hypotheses is a measure of relationship, often called a *correlation coefficient*. There are several, depending upon the level of data you've collected:

Nominal data—χ^2 (chi square) test for independence*
Ordinal data—Spearman rho or Kendall tau
Interval, ratio data—Pearson product moment

The various coefficients can tell you whether a relationship exists, and if so, to what degree. However, care must be taken in the interpretation of correlation coefficients: a relationship between two variables does *not* mean that one variable caused the other.[7] For example, if you computed a correlation coefficient between the students' achievement and attitude toward school at the end of your instructional program, you *cannot* conclude that success in the program brought about a better attitude.

The Pearson product moment correlation coefficient is the most powerful and most commonly used of all the correlation coefficients. By powerful, we mean that if a relationship does exist, you are more likely to detect it with this correlation coefficient than with any of the others.

The kinds of conclusions that are possible and appropriate for any of the correlation coefficients include decisions about relationships, or how two variables are associated. Often it is interesting, and perhaps even important, to know that two things are related. For example, suppose you found a positive relationship between verbal ability and achievement in a reading program. We could conclude that those

---

*The symbol χ^2 is pronounced *chi square*.

with a high level of verbal skills tend to do well in the reading program. Perhaps the reading program requires a high level of verbal ability. And even if this was not your intention in designing the program, that is a useful piece of information. Another possible conclusion is that students who do not do well in the program are those who, in general, have a poor level of verbal ability. Note that none of the statements speaks to causes.

A correlation coefficient can be positive or negative (with the exception of the χ^2), and ranges in value from -1.00 through 0 to $+1.00$. A negative relationship means that as a person's score goes up on one variable, it goes down on the other. You might find a negative relationship, for example, between attendance and achievement in a program. Students who were absent fewer times might achieve a higher score, and students who were absent many times might achieve a lower score. Note that we did not say that poor attendance caused lower achievement. There could have been another factor working here, such as student interest. Less interested students could have attended the program fewer number of times (many absences) and also performed more poorly on the achievement test.

Measures of relationship, such as correlation coefficients, are useful in determining whether two variables are related. You should *never* conclude anything about the causes of the observed relationship. There is a way to determine causation, but it's beyond the scope of this text. We would suggest you consult a research design book and look in the chapters dealing with experimental design.

MEASURING DIFFERENCES

Is the performance of two groups different, or are the scores essentially the same?

Do students score higher on a measure of self-concept after using the Natural Growth materials than students not using these materials?

Is there a higher success rate for job placement after completing a workshop on job application techniques?

There are several techniques useful in answering these questions, but you have three questions to answer, and your answers to these will help determine which statistical technique to use.

First, as was true of the measures of central tendency, variability, and relationship, you will have to be able to specify the *kind of data* you have. *Second,* you will have to state the *number of groups* in the comparison; and *third,* you will have to determine if the groups are related or independent.

Decision Map IV, page 172, is designed to help you answer these questions. The first question, the kind of data, refers to the nominal, ordinal, interval, or ratio level of data. Refer to Decision Map I, page 170, for some extra help.

The number of groups refers to the groups of people involved in the comparison. For example, if all clients participated in the program and you wanted to determine if changes in scores on some particular test were higher at the conclusion of the program, you would have *one group,* with two measures (pretest and posttest). A special name given to this situation (one group, pretest-posttest scores) is a *related group.* If you have only one group, you must have pretest-posttest data to measure changes.

Another example of a related group, this time with two groups, is the case where groups of clients have been matched on several variables such as age, sex, or scores on some tests. Because the groups have been formed in this special way, we call them "related."

The term *independent groups* refers to groups (usually of clients) that are in no way related to one another—no before and after measures, for example. An example of independent groups would be a group of students who had received the instruction and a group of students who had not received the instruction (sometimes called the control or comparison group). You could compare the achievement of these two independent groups after the instruction was delivered to see if the group who received the instruction performed better than the group who did not receive the instruction. Use Decision Map IV to help you select the techniques best suited to your data.

All of the statistical techniques can help you determine whether a difference exists. But don't be overwhelmed by this long list of techniques to look for differences. You answer the three questions, and the answer to these will indicate to you which is the most appropriate way of determining where a difference exists and whether it is significant. Use Decision Map IV, and as you answer each question, move along the map until you "land on" the technique!

All of the computations for these statistical techniques are readily available in various statistical packages on many computers.

Steps in Hypothesis Testing

1. Determine the questions you want answered from the evaluation.
2. Formulate one set of hypotheses for each question.
3. Determine whether the hypotheses are about *differences* or *relationships*.

> If *differences*, see Decision Map IV, page 172, to select test.
> If *relationships*, see Decision Map III, page 171, to select test.

4. Compute the statistical test, using help from statistics books, statistical consultants, and/or computer programs.
5. Determine whether the results are "significant" (see below).

SIGNIFICANT WHAT?

Often a great cheer goes up whenever someone says, "My research is significant." We may not know what that means, but it sounds great! After you compute a relationship or a test of differences, you will have to answer a question: Was this result something that happened by chance, or does the difference or relationship really exist?

One reason for having pairs of hypotheses is the decision to be made about the results: Are they significant (statistically) or not? If the results of the statistical analysis indicate that the result probably did not occur by chance (it was significant), then we reject the null hypothesis and consider the alternate, in this case, that there appeared to be a difference in achievement in mathematics at the conclusion of the program, or, that there was a relationship between completion of the program and successful job placement.

But what if the results are not significant? Then we fail to reject the null hypothesis. (Note that we do *not* accept it; there's a big difference.) If this happens, all we can say is "We don't know if there's a difference or a relationship." We do not have sufficient evidence to say anything else. We cannot say they are the same. Thus, when we fail to reject the null hypothesis, we really don't know too much. And when we do reject it, we know that there is a certain probability (preset by you, the researcher/evaluator) that the result exists and is replicable (repeatable). Thus, statistical significance doesn't really "tell" us anything. All decisions in terms of the program must be made by the researcher/ evaluator. Statistical significance, or the lack of it, is simply a piece of information to be used in interpreting the analyses and in making decisions about the program you're evaluating.

To establish statistical significance you must go through three steps or stages:

1. Set a probability level, called the *alpha level,** which indicates how many times out of 100 results that large or larger will be due to chance. The most commonly used alpha levels are .05 and .01. (Sometimes you will see them referred to as $\alpha = .05$ or $\alpha = .01$.) These mean that if you obtain a particular result and find it is significant at the .05 alpha level, 5 times out of 100 you would get the same result by chance alone, but 95 times out of 100 the difference (or relationship) will really exist. Thus, we may say that this difference is reliable: it would be this large or larger 95 times out of 100 if we were to repeat the study 100 times exactly as we did it originally.

2. Using special tables, determine the value that reflects the .01 or .05 alpha level. These special tables are called *tables of critical values.* The tables reflect these preset probability levels and are designed for your convenience. There are numerous tables of critical values, so be sure you are using the appropriate one. The tables will indicate the size of the difference or the degree of relationship that must exist before it can be considered significant. In whatever statistics book you find the formula, that book also will have the corresponding table of critical values. These tables are tools. Ask for help in using them if you have any questions.

3. Compare your observed (computed) and critical value (from the table). In most cases the decision rule is as follows: If your observed value is equal to or greater than the critical value from the table, then your results are significant.

Let's take an example, starting with the question to be answered:

Are self-concept scores higher after participation in the Women's Re-Entry Program? Next, write a pair of hypotheses, one null and one alternate.

---

*This is a statistical concept referring to a probability level. You will see this term in many statistics books.

There is no difference in self-concept scores before as compared with after participating in the Women's Re-Entry Workshop.

There is a difference in self-concept scores after participating in the Women's Re-Entry Workshop.

These hypotheses are concerned with differences, so we turn to Decision Map IV, page 172. Since the data we have are scores from a measure of self-concept, we can assume we have interval level data.

The next question on the Decision Map concerns the number of groups. We have one group, with a measure of self-concept before and after the program. For one group, with pretest-posttest data, the appropriate statistical test is a "related sample *t* test."

The next step is to compute the statistical data, using whatever resources you have available. For the purpose of our example, let us assume that 25 people completed the program, and that the "answer" we got when we used the formula for a related sample *t* test was 2.83. (Since this text is not a statistics book, you will have to accept our assumptions so we can continue with the example and help you understand what the "answer" means.)

We have reproduced a small part of the table of critical values for the *t* test.

	alpha values		
degrees of freedom	.10	.05	.01
24	1.318	1.711	2.492

(Note: The appropriate number of degrees of freedom will be given with the formula. Here it is $n-1$, or 24. The discussion of the concept of degrees of freedom is beyond the scope of this evaluation text.)

Reviewing the three steps to determine the statistical significance we have the following:

1. Set a probability level, a researcher's decision. For our example, we'll use $\alpha = .05$.

2. Using the table of critical values, identify the appropriate critical value. For $\alpha = .05$, the value is 1.711.

3. Compare the observed (computed) value (ours was 2.83) and the critical value (ours was 1.711).

The decision rule: If the observed value is equal to or greater than the critical value, reject the null hypothesis.

Our decision: Since the observed value of 2.83 is greater than the critical value of 1.711, we reject the null hypothesis and consider the alternate as viable: There *is* a difference in self-concept scores at the end of the workshop.

By inspecting our data, we noted that the mean (average) posttest self-concept score was higher than the mean pretest score. Thus, our results are statistically significant, and we can conclude that the self-concept scores of those people who participated in the workshop scored significantly higher at the end of the program.

STATISTICAL SIGNIFICANCE AND PRACTICAL IMPORTANCE

So what do you know when you find that your results are significant? You know that they are probably not occurring by chance . . . and that's all! Statistical significance is really just a probability statement and, by itself, doesn't mean much at all. Some researchers will try to tell you that because something is statistically significant, it's *very* important. But that's not necessarily true.

Statistical significance and practical importance are two separate issues. One deals with a *probability statement,* and the other deals with a *value judgment.* Practical importance is something the researcher determines. How important is the result? What does it mean in terms of your evaluation project? Statistical significance is not the be-all and end-all of research. Practical importance—the researcher's informed judgment of the meaning of the results—is often much more meaningful in terms of deciding what is (and what is not) happening as a result of the program you've set out to evaluate.

In the above example, we found that there were statistically significant gains in self-concept scores among those participating in the Women's Re-Entry Workshop. The practical importance of this result is that it looks as if the program is effective in helping participants to feel good about themselves—a very important element in any job training and placement program.

INTERPRETING RESULTS OF RELATIONSHIP STUDIES

If your hypotheses concerned relationships rather than differences, these same concepts of statistical significance and practical importance still apply. You decide whether the results are important and meaningful—the practical importance.

A common mistake in interpreting a correlation coefficient is to talk about causation. A relationship between two variables does *not* mean that one variable caused another. For example, if a high degree of relationship was noted between temperature and the use of hammocks, we *cannot* conclude that the higher temperature caused the hammocks to appear. Nor can we conclude that the presence and/or use of hammocks caused the temperature to increase.

Another example can be drawn from program evaluation. Suppose we find that a positive attitude is related to a low absence rate during the instructional program. (Remember, this would be a negative relationship: a "high" score or positive attitude "goes with" a fewer number of absences.) Can we say the good attendance record caused the positive attitude? No! Just because the two variables are related does not mean that one caused the other.

In this case, another variable, perhaps interest in the topic, would account for or explain this relationship. Students who are interested in the topic are more likely to attend classes and also to have a better or more positive attitude than students who are less interested. Note that we are not saying that interest caused this relationship, but that all three variables are probably related.

Relationships do not say anything about cause, and we must be careful in interpreting correlation coefficients. It's important to know what variables are related. Statements about relationships can give us important information about what's happening in the program. So, relationships are important, and we should take care in communicating the results.

USING RESULTS FOR MAKING DECISIONS

Practical importance has to do with how important, or meaningful, the results are to you. What do the results mean in terms of your evaluation, and the decisions you must make? For example, you might find that, in a test of relationship, the results were statistically signficant but, because of a very large sample size, the actual degree of relationship was very small. Is this very small degree of relationship important? If you are using this information from this relationship study to make predictions about admission to a program, will this very small coefficient allow you to make accurate predictions? Most of the time, a small coefficient does not allow for accurate predictions, even though the correlation coefficient was statistically significant. Therefore, you would conclude that the practical importance of the relationship was small, and you would probably continue looking for other ways to predict success in your program.

Practical importance is a program developer's or manager's decision. It allows the developer or manager to think about what the results actually mean, regardless of the statistical significance. Sometimes nonsignificant results are more important and more meaningful than results that are statistically significant.

Decision-making is a very important part of evaluation. In fact, we think it's one of the most important. In Chapter 9 we'll give you some help on making decisions and some suggestions for gaining the cooperation of those persons involved in the project so that the changes can take place smoothly.

SUMMARY

Do all of the statistics seem like one garbled mess, completely unintelligible to almost everyone? Does it seem that all the reports of evaluation are full of jargon? A quick glance at a statistics book will leave most people trembling; there are so many symbols and even Greek letters! If you still feel uneasy about some of the points we've covered, hang in there. Hands-on experience with the points we've covered is often the best kind, especially when it comes to making sense out of the results.

The tools described in this chapter are useful in the evaluation process and can help you make statements you want to make as well as facilitate the decision making you want to accomplish. The results can and should make sense and be meaningful, especially to you.

One thing to remember in statistical analysis is to do only those that make sense to you. Don't do any kind of analysis, statistical or otherwise, that doesn't make sense to you. Don't worry if you require some expert help in the early learning stages.

KEY POINTS

Statistics are tools; so you use them, and don't let them use you.

Statistics can help you describe data and make inferences or draw conclusions about your data.

Different statistical techniques are appropriate for different levels or kinds of data (nominal, ordinal, interval, ratio).

If you know what you want to know and what kind of data you have, then you can use the Decision Maps to help you with the selection of the statistical techniques.

Measures of relationship are just that: indicators of whether two things (variables) are related. They do *not* indicate causes.

Correlation coefficients can range from -1.00 through 0, to $+1.00$, indicating degree of relationship (with the exception of the χ^2 *test for independence*).

Correlation coefficients can be negative or positive, indicating the kind of relationship.

Measures of differences can be used to find out whether groups are really different on some measure or test.

Statistical significance is a probability statement; you decide whether significant differences are important and/or meaningful.

The alpha level tells what probability level you're attaching to the results of the statistical tests.

Be sure you understand what you're doing so that you know if the results are reasonable.

There often is more than one "correct" way of analyzing data; don't be upset if other people suggest different analyses.

It's much easier to communicate the results if you understand them.

Know what results are expected. If you get something unexpected, figure out why.

The null hypothesis is a formal statement of the research question in a no-difference form.

Statistical significance is a piece of information that is useful in interpreting results. It doesn't "tell" you anything.

Don't stop the evaluation when the statistical analyses are finished. Do go on and make interpretations, conclusions, and recommendations in terms of the gaps, goals, and objectives stated early in the evaluation process.

Write down what you have learned and what suggestions you have for making the evaluation process better next time. Don't depend on your memory.

DECISION MAP I

Identifying the Scale of Measurement

Can you group your data into categories such as types of animals?

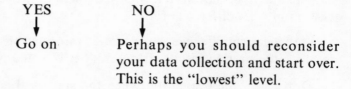

YES   NO

Go on   Perhaps you should reconsider
               your data collection and start over.
               This is the "lowest" level.

Can you rank your data from lowest to highest, best to worst, or form another value judgment on some variable?

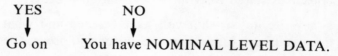

YES   NO

Go on   You have NOMINAL LEVEL DATA.

Can you quantify the distance between students or observations on some variable, such as a math test?

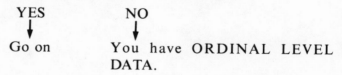

YES   NO

Go on   You have ORDINAL LEVEL
               DATA.

Can you identify a meaningful and absolute zero or beginning point and make meaningful comparisons, such as "twice as much," of some variable?

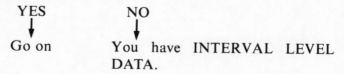

YES   NO

Go on   You have INTERVAL LEVEL
               DATA.

If you have a measurement with equal appearing intervals and a meaningful and absolute beginning place, you have RATIO LEVEL DATA.

DECISION MAP II

Measures of Central Tendency and Variability

If you want to describe the *typical performance*, use a measure of central tendency:

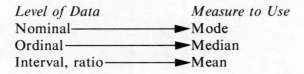

Level of Data   *Measure to Use*
Nominal ————————————► Mode
Ordinal ————————————► Median
Interval, ratio ————————————► Mean

If you want to describe the *variability*, use a measure of variation:

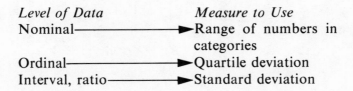

Level of Data   *Measure to Use*
Nominal ————————————► Range of numbers in categories
Ordinal ————————————► Quartile deviation
Interval, ratio ————————————► Standard deviation

DECISION MAP III

Measures of Relationship

If you want to determine relationships:

Level of Data   *Measure to Use**
Nominal ————————————► χ^2 test for independence
Ordinal ————————————► Spearman *rho* or Kendall *tau*
Interval, ratio ————————————► Pearson product moment

*All will yield a correlation coefficient, and all are subject to restrictions in interpretation.

DECISION MAP IV

Measures of Differences

Question I	Question II	Question III		
What level data do I have? (See Decision Map I)	How many groups do I have?	Are the groups independent?	(or)	Are the groups related?
Nominal	1 (pre-post)	No		Yes→McNemar test for changes
	2	No		Yes→McNemar test for changes
	2	Yes→χ^2 test for differences		
	more than 2	No		
	more than 2	Yes→χ^2 test for differences		Yes→Cocharan Q test

Ordinal

1 (pre-post)	No ────────→	Yes→Wilcoxon signed ranks
2	No ────────→	Yes→Wilcoxon signed ranks
2	Yes→Mann Whitney	
more than 2	No ────────→	Yes→Friedman anova
more than 2	Yes→Kruskal-Wallis anova	

Interval ratio

1 (pre-post)	No ────────→	Yes→ t test for related samples
2	No ────────→	Yes→ t test for related samples
2	Yes→ t test for independent samples	
more than 2	No ────────→	Yes→repeated measures anova
more than 2	Yes→anova (analysis of variance)	

Selected References

1. McCall, R. B. *Fundamental Statistics for Psychology.* 2nd ed. New York: Harcourt Brace Jovanovich, 1975.
2. Egan, A. L. *Anxiety-free Statistics.* Dubuque, Iowa: Kendall/Hunt, 1977.
3. Stevens, S. S. "Scales of Measurement." In J. A. Steger, *Readings in Statistics.* New York: Holt, Rinehart & Winston, 1971.
4. Kerlinger, F. N. *Foundations of Behavioral Research.* 2nd ed. New York: Holt, Rinehart & Winston, 1973.
5. Egan, A. L., and DiBartolo, R. *Research: The Magical Mystery Trip.* Dubuque, Iowa: Kendall/Hunt, 1976.
6. Nunnally, J. C. *Introduction to Statistics for Psychology and Education.* New York: McGraw-Hill, 1975.
7. Ennis, R. "On Causality." *Educational Researcher* 2 (1973): 6.
8. Williamson, J. B., Karp, D. A., and Dalphin, J. R. *The Research Craft.* Boston: Little, Brown, 1977.
9. Gay, L. R. *Educational Research: Competencies for Analysis and Application.* Columbus, Ohio: C. E. Merrill, 1976.
10. Asher, J. W. *Educational Research and Evaluation Methods.* Boston: Little, Brown, 1976. (See Chapter 11), "Common Errors in Research."
11. Siegel, S. *Nonparametric Statistics for the Behavioral Sciences.* New York: McGraw-Hill, 1956.
12. Winer, B. J. *Statistical Principles in Experimental Design.* New York: McGraw-Hill, 1962.

8
IMPLEMENTING THE EVALUATION

You should have, by this time, determined *what* it is you want to evaluate, *why* you want to evaluate it, for *whom* the evaluation is designed, what evaluation *model* to use, or how to choose one, and what *data* you will have to collect. Now is the time to conduct the actual evaluation procedure, collect the data, conduct the analyses, make the decisions and recommendations, and write the final report.

But before you plunge into it, *stop!* Should you (or will you have to) do it alone?

COMMITMENTS HELP

Now that you've invested so much time and energy in the evaluation, you might want to stop at this point and ask, "Whose evaluation is it?" We are assuming that you have been working closely with the program developers, the teachers, and various other members of the agency. If it is decided it's their evaluation, let them read this book and see how important commitment is. You may be doing an excellent job as manager and planner of the evaluation, but unless other key people are committed to the project and willing to work to implement the recommended changes, nothing may happen as a result of all your work.

Assuming you did the needs assessment correctly, you will have identified those persons who are committed to the evaluation project. You will also know who the various audiences are and what they are working for as a result of the needs assessment. It is good to involve key people in the planning phases throughout the evaluation process. There may be a variety of audiences, including the participants, their families, program support staff, members of the community, policy makers and other officials, funding agencies, and perhaps even legislative bodies. These all are potential partners in the evaluation effort. Each type of audience, however, may identify a slightly different set of questions to be addressed. Thus it is important to identify the audiences for which the evaluation is designed and to include members of these groups as partners in planning and in the evaluation.

As you plan, involve your partners in identifying the specific questions to be addressed. Although you may be considered responsible for the overall evaluation project, a close working relationship with your partners will help ensure that the issues they're interested in are addressed and that they feel they are a part of the evaluation effort. If changes in the evaluation process are suggested, they should be carefully substantiated in the manner in which your evaluation plan has been derived. Don't make changes on the basis of "getting togetherness" or to placate someone in the group. Evaluation is important, it is objective, and it is critical that you do not compromise the results by changing your design and procedures for social or political reasons alone. Be sure that any changes make sense. Assure yourself that the changes will provide better answers to the evaluation questions and meet the objectives of the evaluation.

The partnership arrangement should help facilitate the implementing of the recommendations made as a result of the evaluation of the program. Thus, an important part of the evaluation process is the inclusion of other key people. But you can facilitate their cooperation and commitment. Although involving your partners in the entire process of evaluation may be time-consuming (in terms of the time involved in attending meetings, and so on) in the long run, it should help with the implementation of changes as indicated by the results of the evaluation. And if the results and changes aren't implemented, what good was the evaluation? Get your partners involved so that they can "go" with the results!

RESOURCES: DON'T SKIMP

The most important resources in implementing the evaluation process are the ones you can actually use to help you accomplish the evaluation. Identifying and being able to use existing resources may keep the cost of the evaluation down. Money spent on evaluation cannot also be spent on delivering or improving the program.

- How do you know for sure that a particular resource is or is not available?
- Have you done a thorough and careful inventory of resources?
- What or who have you identified that is available to help you with, for example, the data collection and analysis?
- Does the agency have a standard testing program of some sort, such as an intake assessment?
- If so, will any of these tests be useful in collecting data for the evaluation?
- Could those conducting the testing program administer some of the tests you've designed or selected and help with the data collection process?
- Is there a computer available for you to use for the data analysis?

- Will you have the assistance of a computer consultant?
- Could others help you with the actual data analysis after you've completed the collection of data?
- Have you considered employing an outside contractor for parts of the evaluation, especially some of the analyses?

If the district or agency has no computer facilities available, perhaps you could hire a person from a nearby university to run the computer for you. You might also consider an outside contractor for other parts of the evaluation, such as designing and pilot testing some of the instruments. However, it is important to know what the contractor is doing. If she or he is working on the data analysis, be sure the questions you want answered are being addressed.

Don't try to do everything yourself. Rely on others for help during the various phases of the evaluation. Of course, you'll have to know who can do what, and what's available, before others can help you. Early in the evaluation process, make an inventory of your resources and determine the relative costs. Find out what's available, who can do what, who's willing to help with the project, and what the costs are. If you don't know the *who, what,* and *where,* you may be ignoring—and wasting—a lot of valuable resources.

PLANNING THE IMPLEMENTATION OF THE EVALUATION PLAN

Once you've identified your partners and are sure they're committed to the evaluation process, if you have identified and inventoried your resources, you are ready for the implementation of the evaluation plan. Have you written your plan? You may know exactly what you're going to do, when you're going to do it, and who's available to help you during the entire process. Great! You've done well in applying the ideas presented in earlier chapters. But you must write the plan out. Any plan that stays in your head is difficult to communicate effectively to other people, and it sometimes becomes inconsistent and hard to follow. If you've already done all that work, do this one more small thing—write it down. That way you won't have problems remembering the order of events, and others will know exactly what you're up to also. (It's easier to get cooperation if everything is "on the table" and there's no hidden agenda.) Sometimes people feel threatened by an evaluation, especially if they don't know exactly what you're up to or don't understand it.

ITEMS TO HAVE IN HAND

It's a good idea to work from lists so that you know exactly where you are and where you're going. Here are the items you should now have:

1. *The goals and objectives for the program, project, or intervention you are to evaluate.* (If you have been thorough, you will also have justification for these goals and objectives in terms of what they are to contribute outside the agency for which you work—in society.) These goals and objectives should preferably be measurable on an interval or ratio scale, and they should be categorized as to whether they deal with inputs, processes, products, outputs, and/or outcomes.

2. *Questions that should be answered by the evaluation if all the processes and procedures are successfully implemented.* These questions should be carefully framed and should reflect exactly what the evaluation is to accomplish—the story it should tell. For example, questions might be as follows:

- Did the learners master the objectives?
- What contribution did this program make in terms of increasing the reading ability of third grade children in the district?
- Was the value added to society significantly increased by this program?
- Did the job placement program help to increase the

number of displaced homemakers finding and obtaining employment?

- Did the workshop measurably improve the assertive behavior of those participating?
- Was client self-concept improved as a result of this activity?

There are several reasons (good ones, we think) to plan ahead so that you will know where you are going and will be able to tell when you are there. Careful preplanning and specifying the questions to be answered by the evaluation will:

- *assure you that your evaluation methods and means are appropriate and correct,*
- *assure those who will be using the evaluation data that the information resulting from the evaluation process will be useful to them in making the appropriate decisions, and*
- *identify gaps in the evaluation design which must be "plugged" before implementing the evaluation process. (If gaps are found, such as not controlling for differences in entry-level mastery, you can identify possible evaluation tools and techniques to answer the questions formerly excluded.)*

3. *The goals and objectives of your evaluation.* These should be directly keyed, or related, to specific questions you want to answer, and you should know what you want to do with the answers to those questions.

4. *The selection of and written statement of the type of evaluation model you will use.* Make sure you know exactly what is expected, what it is you will be required to do, when you will be required to do it, and what you will be delivering when you are through. Again, check with the list of questions you have developed to assure yourself that the evaluation model (or sections of it) will provide the answers to those questions. If it will not, then you must revise your plans.

5. *The types of data you will be gathering.* The data are used to provide the evidence upon which judgments are made. Some of the questions identified will require data consisting of test scores or results from scales or surveys. These are called *quantitative data,* and may be of the ordinal or interval levels we discussed earlier. It is these types of data for which the statistical analyses are done and for which concerns of reliability and validity are important.

However, there are other types of evidence that may be useful in determining the value of the program. These are *qualitative* or *descriptive data,* which may include descriptions of the program, the community, or the participants. Other types of qualitative data include anecdotes, impressions, and observations. These data cannot be quantified, forced into categories and numbers, and submitted to computer analysis. They are important, however, in providing a complete picture of the program being evaluated.

6. *A list of the statistical tools you will be using.* Again, compare these tools, their characteristics and uses, with your questions and evaluation objectives. Will these statistical techniques provide the answers? Are these tools appropriate to the types of data you have and to the number of groups you will be working with?

Since the selection of the statistical tools presents a stumbling block to many people, we've included the following review to help you know "which tools to use when" as you are implementing your evaluation plan.

WHICH TOOLS TO USE WHEN

How do you know which tools to use in your evaluation? The tools you selected are in part dependent upon the evaluation model (or the portions) you select and exactly what you want to find out.

Where in the whole program planning and development process do you want to be able to make statements?

- During the planning phase?
- During the installation phase?
- During the implementation phase?
- After the program has been completed?

If this is your first attempt at program evaluation, and if you don't have a large staff or a significant commitment of time and staff from the school district or other agency, perhaps you should limit your efforts to one, or possibly two, phases of the whole program development process. Biting off a large chunk, or trying to do a large-scale comprehensive evaluation the first time around may prove to be an overwhelming and unwieldy task, and you may have more problems and mistakes to learn from than you'd really like to have. So start small. Decide exactly what's important to know about now. It's a good feeling to be able to build on success.

Let's say you want to make statements about the products, or outputs, of the program. You can't wait until the program is completed to begin the evaluation process. Rather, you should be working with the program planners and developers from the very beginning. Are you going to want to make statements about changes in behavior, attitudes, or knowledge as a result of this program? The best way to measure change is to know what the attitudes, behaviors, and knowledge of the participants were at the beginning of the program. Thus, data must be collected before the participants are exposed to any of the program materials. How can you measure change or impact if you don't know what was happening before the program began? Sometimes this is called *baseline-data* because it gives us data describing what's going on before the program to use as a basis of comparison with what has happened as a result of the program.

After you have decided what kinds of statements you want to make (or the agency decides with you just what it is they want to know), your next step is to identify the variables (attitudes, behaviors, skills, and knowledge, and so forth) that will be measured.

Let's say you are interested in determining whether the math skills program facilitates positive attitudes toward math and lessens anxiety about math and numbers. You also want to know whether positive attitudes toward math are related to doing well and having a low level of anxiety, to the point of enrolling in a technical job preparation program.

In order to know whether an attitude becomes more positive, you have to know what the attitude was before the math skills program began. The same is true of anxiety. How anxious were the clients about math before the program began? You will have to have a *before measure,* or base-line data, before you can establish whether any changes took place.

We have identified four variables here:
- attitudes toward math,
- anxiety about math,
- achievement in math,
- enrollment in a technical job preparation program.

You know the program has been designed for persons who have been out of the job market for some time, so you will have to pay particular attention to the level of reading difficulty for the various instruments you consider (in addition to the concerns we've talked about already: reliability, validity, and level of measurement).

Your inventory of local resources has indicated that the agency routinely collects data relating to past employment history as well as general aptitude and achievement information. Since a math skills subtest is a part of the battery, you will be able to use already existing data, and not spend time or effort to collect additional achievement data for the pretest data.

A review of the literature has revealed several possibilities for the attitude and anxiety instruments, so you write to the publishers and/or authors to obtain copies of the instrument and the test manual. After receiving the instruments and carefully examining them, you find two that appear to meet your requirements. You note that all three instruments (the achievement test and the two you selected) will give you interval level data. Enrollment in the technical job preparation program is on the nominal level: yes or no.

The three instruments are administered in the fall before the program begins, and again in the spring after the program is finished. In the fall the enrollment data are collected. Okay, we have the data. Now what? Now you have to choose the statistical techniques that will help provide the information necessary to make the decisions about the impact and effectiveness of the program.

SO YOU HAVE TO USE SOME STATISTICS

Details of the calculation of some of the most commonly used statistics are included in any of the standard statistical references at the end of Chapter 7. But before you (or your team members) can use these formulas, you will have to decide which ones to use. Let's go back to the questions we wanted to ask about the math skills program. The first was: Does the math skills program facilitate positive attitudes toward math? The pair of hypotheses for this question is:

There is no difference in attitudes toward math at the end of the program.

There is a difference in attitudes toward math at the end of the program.

Going to Decision Map I (page 170), we first have to identify the level of data. Earlier, we mentioned that all three instruments would give us interval level data. Therefore, the level of data is interval, and the number of groups is one, with before and after measures. Now, turn to Decision Map IV (page 172). With interval level data, and before and after measures on one group, we see that the appropriate statistical test is the related sample t test.

The second question is similar to the first: Does the math skills program lessen anxiety about math and numbers?

The hypotheses are:
- There is no difference in math anxiety after the program.
- There is a difference in math anxiety after the program.

Here we have interval data also, with before and after measures on one group. Thus, we should use the related sample t test as for the first question.

The third question deals with a relationship: Is there a positive relationship between attitudes toward math and achievement? That is, do those clients who do well in math also have a positive attitude toward it? The hypotheses are:

There is no relationship between achievement in and attitude toward math.

There is a relationship between achievement in and attitude toward math.

Since this question deals with relationships, turn to Decision Map III (page 171). With interval level data, the appropriate measure is the Pearson Product Moment Correlation Coefficient.

The fourth question is similar to the third in that it deals with relationships but different in that it asks about a negative relationship: Do clients who earn high scores on the math achievement test have a low level of anxiety about math and numbers? The hypotheses are:
- There is no relationship between achievement and anxiety in math.
- There is a relationship between achievement and anxiety in math.

Since we have interval level data, the Pearson Product Moment Correlation Coefficient is the appropriate statistical technique to use. (The various correlation coefficients are used to compute both negative and positive correlations, with the exception of the χ^2.)

The fifth question deals with enrollment in a technical job preparation program: Do clients with low math anxiety tend to enroll in technical job preparation programs? The hypotheses are:

- There is no relationship between math anxiety and enrollment in a technical job preparation program.
- There is a relationship between math anxiety and enrollment in a technical job preparation program.

Since the enrollment data are nominal (yes-no), we'll also form categories for the anxiety scores so that we will have high and low groups. These are nominal level variables then, and to determine the relationship between enrollment in the job preparation program and anxiety, we would use the χ^2 test for independence.

If you have determined that you are the one who will do the actual computations, find another person to do them also as a cross-check. (Incidentally, this is called *reliability*: are both of you consistently getting the same results?) It would be quite embarrassing to draw conclusions based on erroneous data because of mathematical errors.

If, on the other hand, your list of resources has indicated the availability of computers, work closely with the computer operator to be sure that no clerical errors enter into the evaluation process.

No matter which way you do it, take one step at a time. It's just like balancing a checkbook and you should do it slowly and carefully.

Now you have your tools with you and your plans carefully laid out. You are satisfied that the questions for which you seek answers will be answered. It is now your job to get the answers.

DELIVERING WHAT WAS PLANNED

In order to get an evaluation plan implemented and completed, you will have to have people, resources, time, and data. In addition, you will have to convert the data (raw results and summaries of results) into information (data which are useful) for making decisions.

People. Work *with* people. Let them know what it is you

want to do and why you want to do it. Speak *with* them, not *at* them. Remember that programs are people, and the people who are being evaluated are usually concerned that they will be judged. Many people feel, deep down, that they might be found wanting. Assure them that evaluation is not a blame-placing procedure and that, if changes are suggested as a result of the evaluation, these will be system changes that the people themselves would probably agree with. Remember that change and evaluation are painful for most people, so be gentle.

In working with people, be absolutely clear about

- *what each one is to do,*
- *what each one is responsible for delivering,*
- *when each person is to deliver each product for which he or she is responsible,*
- *what resources each person will have in order to produce his or her product, and*
- *what quality standards will be used to judge the acceptability for each product.*

You should set up a time and event chart that shows this information:

PROJECT DEADLINE

Project Elements/ Products	Due Dates	Actually Delivered	Comments
1.			
2.			
(etc.)			

With such a chart, you and others can keep track of what is due, when it is due, and what the status of each element is at any time during the evaluation process. Follow the chart, and ask in advance if things are on schedule.

Impress upon all your co-workers the importance of

- *quality (reliability and validity of results), and*
- *timelines (getting things done when they are supposed to be done).*

People tend to let things slide and then rush at the last minute; as a result, the product quality suffers. Try to get a joint commitment to the evaluation process and evaluation plan.

Be sure to praise good work and to give encouragement when appropriate. When you notice that work is not of the quality necessary or is not being done on time, don't criticize or blame. Instead, provide help, support, guidance, and assistance. Be open about progress and problems, and share these. Frequently, your co-workers can come up with some good ideas for licking the tough problems or removing the stumbling blocks you've encountered. When considering changes, however, make sure that you are not compromising the design, integrity, and correctness of the data you are collecting. Be ready to change, but make absolutely sure that the changes are in the best interest of answering the questions you seek to answer through the evaluation.

Nonhuman resources. The physical tools with which you have to work are your nonhuman resources. Usually the resources (other than people) have to do with money or budget. List your resources. Make sure they will do the jobs that have to be done. If they will not, "trade them in" for some that will.

List the resources required for each of the products to be produced. Put the resources on a timeline, such as the one on the facing page. You might place this on a large wall chart.

Project Element/Product
1.
2.
(etc.)
Month (from beginning 1 2 3 4 5 6 7 8 9 and so forth, of project)
Resources required:
Personnel required:

By noting when resources (including people) will be required by month and by each project element/product, you can easily see the *loadings,* the requirements for personnel and resources for each time period for each project element/product. If you have too many people or resources, you can reduce the number. If you have too few of one or both, you can reassign. Be a planner, stick to your plan (or revise it as required), and know where you are going. A good plan will see you through most problems.

Time. Time is the duration of your evaluation project. Use it wisely. By doing what is suggested above, you will know what it is that you are doing, what you have available to do it with (resources, both material and people), and when each element/product is due.

If you are a poor time manager (if time seems to slip away from you or if there always seems to be things undone which should have been completed) try doing the following:

Make a list of everything that has to be done each day. Arrange these things in priority order. Start doing them. At the end of the day, survey your accomplishments and cross off the list the things completed. Do this every day, and do not carry over items from one day to the next; make each list anew each day.

If items are important, they will show up in subsequent lists. Keep charting your accomplishments and your delays on the time and event chart. Know what is going on, what is on schedule, and what is behind schedule. Take steps to get things in on time. But make sure you do not set up artificial deadlines; each deadline should be real and important, not arbitrary. Don't put "safety cushions" in your time estimates without telling your co-workers. They know what is realistic and what is not, and by being honest, you will maintain their respect.

Data. Data are what you want to collect. Make sure that each product that you are obtaining yields the data you want. Make sure they are collected in the way in which they were to be collected, and make sure that they are exactly what you require.

Double-check each product, and double-check each product plan to assure that you will get what you set out to get. Don't ever fudge any data. Even if something has really gone badly and the data are awful, don't try to clean them up. Find some way to re-collect the data, or omit them from your study. Reporting data which are not "real" will lead decision makers to make decisions based on incomplete or incorrect data. Don't fudge even a little. *None.*

If the quantitative data are to be machine scored, or processed, put them into the machine when they are scheduled to be processed. In the meantime, keep them in a secure place where they cannot be lost or tampered with. When they are being processed, make some independent checks on the results to make sure the correct routine or data analysis procedures were used. (Yes, data specialists and computer people do make mistakes.)

Keep track of all the products and data by category. Know where everything is all of the time. The data are the heart of the evaluation; they form the input to your analysis, recommendations, and conclusions. The data have to be good. They are the basis for the decisions and recommendations you'll be making.

A very important part of the evaluation is making decisions, drawing conclusions, and making recommendations about what should happen as a result of the evaluation. Many times agency officials and other decision makers will turn right to the results, discussion, and conclusions section of your report to see what the whole thing means.

But how do you approach the decision making process?

The place to start is with the needs assessment and evaluation plan. What gaps were identified? Was the information gathered to address the gaps and determine how these gaps were being filled? Hopefully the data collected will provide the information necessary to make statements about the gaps.

You may wish to place the information gathered in the needs assessment, the kind of data you've collected, and the results of the analyses of the data into three lists. That way, you'll have all the information right there in front of you as you formulate statements that reflect the conclusions, interpretations and recommendations you make on the basis of the evaluation.

Results from Needs Assessment	Data Gathered	Results of Analyses
68% of the teachers are certified in reading; 90% should be.	Teacher-competency-in-reading test was administered.	After in-service reading program, 85% passed the competency test.
Children should be able to spell on at least a third grade level.	Spelling test Performance	At the end of the program, the mean score was 2.9 grade level, as compared with 2.6 before. This difference was significant.
26% of women returning to the job market seek technical jobs; 60% should seek such jobs because they're better paying than others.	Job placement data	After a counseling program, 58% of the women sought and obtained technical jobs.

Be sure that all of your statements make sense to you. It's difficult to communicate and explain results you don't understand.

FORMULATING YOUR REPORT

Communicating the results of your evaluation is a very important aspect of the entire process. Thus, the format of the final report is very important. It should stand for itself, and speak well for the work you have done, with no additional defense or interpretation necessary from you. In general, there is a standard order for any research or evaluation report. Therefore, your concern will be clarity of communication within these sections.

Sections you might want to provide include:
1. Executive summary of results
2. Introduction
3. Statement of purpose
4. Description of methodology
5. Results and discussion
6. Conclusions and recommendations

Executive summary of results. An executive summary will provide a brief synopsis of the important results that were obtained and their implications. This is for the busy person who might not read the full report or might just skim it.

Introduction. This section will include a brief overview of the area of concern and a justification and rationale for the problem selected for study. The results of the needs assessment should be presented here, and the specific problems selected for study should be identified in such a way as to be able to relate them to the organizational elements model.

Statement of purpose. This section includes the general statement of purpose of the evaluation, as well as the specification of the objectives to be addressed. The objectives should be narrow enough and concrete enough to indicate the kind of data necessary to address each.

Description of methodology. This section will include a description of who was studied (patients, teachers, or whatever), exactly how the data were collected, what model was selected for the evaluation, and what analyses were done. The information should be presented in enough detail so that others could use your report as a guide if they wanted to do the study again.

Results and discussion. What was found as a result of the statistical tests you used? What does it all mean? This section will include an actual reporting of these statistical results, including tables as required, decisions based on these analyses regarding the hypotheses, and a discussion of what all of this means.

Conclusions and recommendations. This section contains the decisions made based on the evaluation, and a specific set of recommendations for action to be taken as a result of the evaluation.

As you write the conclusions and recommendations section, keep asking yourself these questions:

- *Are my statements clear?*
- *Do they provide the answers requested by those who helped plan the evaluation?*
- *Can the appropriate decisions be made based on my statements?*
- *If some gaps are still there, or if the statements cannot be made, why is that?*
- *What are some of the possible shortcomings in the evaluation process?*

In preparing your report, you should keep in mind that evaluation includes *valuation.* Not only do we want to measure the extent to which we accomplished that which we set out to accomplish, but we also want to determine the value of that which occurred.

In your report, note not only the effects—the results in terms of what was intended to happen as compared with what did happen, but also answer the question "So what?"

- *Did what happened become worthwhile to those concerned?*
- *Was the effort worth the investment of time, money, and people?*
- *Did it make a difference that was important to other people, or just to those doing the study?*
- *What did the recipients gain from the study?*

The report is designed to communicate. There are often several versions of the report of the evaluation. The most common are *external,* or the positive outcomes of the program highlighted for public relations, and *internal,* or a critical determination of both the positive and negative impact designed for those who will redesign the program. Although the specific audiences for the results of the evaluation should be identified during the planning stages since the information requirements of audiences vary, it is still possible to communicate results to diverse audiences by changing the writing style and/or emphasis.

WHEN THINGS GO WRONG

Go wrong? Of course, something always does. Be ready for it. The best laid plans often go awry. When something does go wrong, find out what it is, and why it happened. You want to know what went wrong, not to place blame, but to enable you to determine what to do to correct the error. In some cases, it only requires a shift in schedule, or a discussion with someone to negotiate a change or modification in resources.

If it is in the data collection process or results, then you have something of a different nature. You cannot talk or negotiate the problem away. If the data are destroyed, if they are not usable, then realize it and know that you will have to collect the data again or do without them.

Obviously, re-collection is better, but some evaluation designs and procedures mitigate against that: you cannot

give a group another pretest when they have already pro-
gressed to the point of learning or when the intervention
you were evaluating has already changed their pretest behavior.

There are some statistical techniques in which some
kinds of blunders can be partially or fully overcome. Check
with a consultant since these techniques are often quite
complex. The other choice is doing without the data. However, do this only when you have checked with an evaluation
specialist and all else has failed.

The critical points to remember are that you have to
use faithful data; there can be no changes, no variations in
what you set out to get. If you do make changes, make sure
you have a solid rationale for them and report them in the
evaluation results. If you do careful planning and follow
your plan, these kinds of problems will not happen very
often.

Even if you feel that the whole evaluation process went
fairly smoothly, there is probably still room for improvement. In addition to providing information for decision
makers and/or making the decision yourself, you will find
that the evaluation process can be a learning experience for
you and others involved. Don't just drop things once the
data are analyzed, the conclusions drawn, and the statements
made. Go over the entire evaluation process, each part of it,
beginning with the initial planning.

- *Was the planning adequate?*
- *Was there a satisfactory degree of commitment
  and cooperation on the part of important people,
  such as teachers, parents, school administrators,
  clients, and agency directors?*
- *Were the resources adequate?*
- *Did the resource people who agreed to help really
  come through?*
- *How could the data collection have been done
  more smoothly?*

As you think about each and every step of the whole process, ask yourself these questions:

- *How could things have been made better?*
- *What have I learned for next time?*

Do more than just think about these things. Write down your suggestions so that next time you participate in an evaluation, you can benefit from your experiences. It's okay to make honest mistakes; we all do. The important thing is to learn from those mistakes and make things better the next time.

KEY POINTS

- In order for the evaluation to accomplish what you want it to accomplish, you must plan.
- The elements with which you have to work are people, physical resources, time, and data.
- People should be made a part of the evaluation, not the target of it.
- Understand that people who are being evaluated should be assured that it is not a blame-placing process.
- People working with you should be listened to and involved in the evaluation planning as well as the doing.
- Never change the evaluation plan or tools and procedures in order to placate an individual; changes should always be made in order to improve the quality of the resulting evaluation information.
- You as the evaluator make decisions about the statistical results and suggest implications for the results.
- In order to choose the appropriate statistical technique, you must know exactly what questions you want to answer.
- Limit the number of questions you want to answer. Start small so that you will have a better chance of being successful.
- Select instruments to measure the variables you've iden-

tified, paying particular attention to the reliability, validity, and level of measurement.

- Physical resources should be allocated to products to be achieved.
- A formal time and event status chart should be made. It should show:
  Products to be produced
  People assignments and "loadings"
  Physical resource assignments and "loadings"
  Time to be completed and time actually completed
  Status notes
- Make sure that your evaluation plan and evaluation procedures exactly match:
  Evaluation of the project or program
  Intervention goals and objectives
  Questions to be answered by the evaluation
  Goals and objectives of the evaluation
- When something goes wrong (and something always will), be ready to make reasonable and responsible changes, but never compromise the quality of the data.
- Never make any changes that will attack the validity and usefulness of the data.
- Report any unexpected events in your evaluation report.
- Learn from what went right and from what went wrong.

Selected References

1. Argyris, C. "Creating Effective Research Relationships in Organizations." In *Readings in Evaluation Research,* edited by F. G. Caro. New York: Russell Sage Foundation, 1971.
2. Lawrence, P. R. "How to Deal with Resistance to Change." *Harvard Business Review* 32 (1954): 49–57.
3. Cohen, D. K. "Politics and Research." In E. R. House, *School Evaluation: The Politics and Process.* Berkeley, Calif.: McCutchan, 1973.

4. Corey, S. M. *Action Research to Improve School Practices.* New York: Columbia University Press, 1953.
5. Weiss, C. H. *Evaluation Research: Methods of Assessing Program Effectiveness.* Englewood Cliffs, N.J.: Prentice-Hall, 1972.
6. Schulberg, H. C., and Baker, F. "Program Evaluation Models and the Implementation of Research Findings." In *Readings in Evaluation Research,* edited by F. G. Caro. New York: Russell Sage Foundation, 1971.
7. Rutman, L. "Planning an Evaluation Study." In *Evaluation Research Models: A Basic Guide,* edited by L. Rutman. Beverly Hills, Calif.: Sage, 1977.
8. Andrew, G. "Some Observations on Management Problems in Applied Social Research." *The American Sociologist* 2 (1967): 84–89, 92.

9
INTERPRETING AND ACTING
UPON THE RESULTS

Making sense of the results of your evaluation, or of someone else's, is an important first step in making changes. In this chapter, we will give you some help in reading and interpreting the results of the evaluation, in deciding upon the usefulness of the results, and in taking action to bring about the changes recommended by the evaluation. The ideas presented in this chapter should be useful to the program evaluator who has been responsible for the design and implementation of the evaluation process, as well as to the project manager who must make the programmatic decisions and formulate the action plan. To be useful, the results must be understandable to the intended audience. A report that is very technical and very complete might be found relatively useless because those who are responsible for implementing the recommendations may not understand the technical terms.

READING AND UNDERSTANDING
EVALUATION REPORTS

Most evaluations include a final report, describing what has been done and what the recommendations for change (or no change) were. A good report will specify these things clearly, and the reader will be left with few questions concerning the why, how, and what next. These are four questions that must be clearly addressed. These include:

- Why was this particular problem selected for study?
- What was the purpose of the evaluation?
- Do the evaluators or program personnel appear to have accomplished this purpose?
- What recommendations were made on the basis of the evaluation?

Let's look at each of these questions and see what kind of information should be available to address each.

WHY WAS THIS PARTICULAR PROBLEM SELECTED FOR STUDY?

This is the needs assessment question, which is aimed at documenting the gaps that have been selected for resolution and at building a rationale for the selection of this particular problem. In any report, there should be a justification of the problem selected for study. The problem, or the gap, should be phrased in such a way as to make it possible to identify where in the organizational elements model the problem lies. Is this problem the *overall* problem, or is it a symptom of a larger one? Let's look at an example:

> *There was a continuing increase in dropouts from the Scenic School District, starting in 1972 at 42 percent of all students and continuing on an upward trend through last year, when the figure reached 61 percent. This problem was judged by the school board to be of first priority for resolution. The decision was to evaluate the instructional program to determine what might be the cause of the increasing dropout rate.*

Where in the organizational elements model does this problem fall? It is not input since it does not deal with goals, objectives, or the incoming skills, knowledge, and attitudes of learners. It is not directly related to the process since it deals with dropouts, not with the methods-(means)-used in the Scenic School District. It does not deal with product since it is more than the en-route results of the processes used in the school district. Finally, it is not outcome because it tells nothing of the attained level of self-sufficiency of the learners once they have dropped out.

That leaves us with output. The problem statement addresses the question of output since it relates to what happens to learners exiting from the schools—61 percent are dropping out before completing graduation requirements. Since we have discovered where this problem lies in the organizational elements model, we can see its place in the overall picture and consider the question, What about those higher elements? In this case, the one higher element is outcome, and by studying the output element, we might be begging the questions posed by outcome. Questions at this level would include, What percentage of those dropping out were self-sufficient after leaving? Let us again remind you that you do not have to consider every problem statement from the outcome level. Rather, you should be able to identify *where* the problem lies in the organizational elements model and be able to specify what kind of answers will and will not be available.

Here is another example:

For several years, teachers in the Foursquare School have believed that the self-concepts of their students were quite low and that these low self-concepts may be contributing to the low level of achievement among the students at the school. Therefore, it was decided that some effort must be made to increase the self-concepts of these students. The third grade was selected for study, and the Good Feelings materials developed by the Growth Corporation were selected for use. As directed, the students read the materials and made a list of good things about them-

selves. This was done each week for one entire semester in the hope that self-concept, and therefore also the achievement level, would be increased. You are called upon to evaluate the impact of this program at the end of the first semester.

Where in the organizational elements model does this problem fall? There seems to be the greatest concern here with the process, which, if successful, may increase self-concept. However, there was no documentation concerning the actual level of self-concept of the students before the program began (input), nor does there seem to be any data concerning the products (performance or achievement of these students) or for outcomes (how well these students did when they left school).

Thus, there seem to be several unanswered questions, as well as several pieces of missing data. About all you can do at this point is measure the self-concept of the learners and the level of their achievement. Since there are no *before* measures, no comparisons can be made, and the actual impact of the program cannot be truly assessed. Since the problem was stated in terms of the process, there are many issues that cannot be addressed. Perhaps the impact of the program can be inferred through teacher observations of the students' self-concept and level of achievement. However, these observations would be based on the teachers' judgments and on the teachers' memories of the level of student performance and self-concept before the program began.

Therefore, as you read the results of an evaluation such as this, be aware of the many pieces of missing information. If a problem can be phrased in terms of either outcome or output, you are probably dealing with an important problem rather than with a symptom of the problem.

An important aspect of any displaced homemaker program is assisting its clients to become economically self-sufficient. This usually means successful job placement and survival in society. The Urban Displaced Homemaker

*program has been funded by the city council for the past
year, and you have been asked to follow up the graduates
in order to evaluate the effectiveness of the program.*

The concern here is with outcome: to what extent the
graduates were self-sufficient after leaving the program. This
is sometimes considered the ultimate question asked of any
program. You would probably identify the employers of the
graduates and interview them about how well the program
prepared the graduates to be contributors to society. You
might also interview the graduates themselves to determine
their perceptions of their ability to survive.

• WHAT WAS THE PURPOSE OF THE EVALUATION?

The purpose of the evaluation should be a concrete
statement of the specific intents of the evaluation.

Why is the evaluation being done?

What information will be generated? What kinds of
information requirements are there for the decision-making
process?

The statement of purpose often provides an overview of
the concern, and then specific goals and/or objectives are
presented that will provide more specific guidelines for the
evaluation. The statement of purpose will provide you with
information as to the intent of the evaluation and should
reflect both the problem selected for resolution and the
justification of that problem.

• DO THE EVALUATORS APPEAR TO HAVE ACCOMPLISHED THIS PURPOSE?

This question is more difficult to answer. Several considerations are necessary, beginning with the selection of the
instruments used to collect the data.

- Will the instruments yield the type of data necessary?
- Are the instruments valid and reliable?

- Are they appropriate (to the reading level of the clients, for example) for the sample being studied?
- On what basis was the evaluation model selected?
- Is the model appropriate to the problem and the overall purpose?
- Do the analyses relate directly to the goals and objectives specified?
- Is each objective/goal addressed by an appropriate statistical analysis?
- Are the results clearly specified?
- Do the recommendations make sense based on the analysis?
- Are both statistical significance and practical importance considered?
- Does it all seem to make sense?
- Is each step clearly specified so that there are no questions about what was done?

In reading and evaluating any final report, each question should be addressed individually. It is not enough to skim through to see that the various topics are mentioned. The readers should be able to understand what happened so that they can make judgments about the value and usefulness of the results and recommendations.

• WHAT RECOMMENDATIONS WERE MADE ON THE BASIS OF THE EVALUATION?

A very important part of evaluation is making a decision based on the data collected and then making recommendations (based on those decisions) for changing, keeping, or dumping the program that's being evaluated. The list of recommendations should be quite specific and should include guidelines for action. Sometimes an implementation plan is also included. This plan gives detailed explanations of how the recommendations will be implemented, including a listing of who will be doing what. The recommendations are the "meat" of the evaluation and may require the contributions and creative suggestions of all those involved in the evaluation. This section is often of great interest to administrators and is usually given a great amount of attention. Questions such as the following are addressed here:

- What differences do the results make to clients?
- What differences do the results make to instructors or others who interact with the clients?
- What differences do the results make for administrators?
- What differences do the results make for community members?
- What differences do the results make in the field?

If the data are available to address these five questions, the reader should have the information necessary to make decisions about the overall quality of the evaluation, as well as the utility of the recommendations.

DECIDING ABOUT THE USEFULNESS OF THE RESULTS

The single most important consideration a person can use in deciding what happens as a result of the evaluation process is the usefulness of the effort—whether or not the activities and procedures are worth the price in terms of costs and results. An evaluation is designed to answer questions and supply information for decisions. Even if the evaluation was well-done and the questions raised were answered, there still is the matter of cost—in staff, time, and money—to be considered in deciding what actually will be done with the results of the evaluation.

Let's look at an example in which the recommendations of the evaluation answered the questions, but the decision was made that the recommendations were too costly to implement.

The Displaced Homemaker Center was evaluated after one year of funding by the city council. It was found that sixty women participated during the year in the various workshops offered by the center. The main goal of the center's various workshops and programs was to help the participants to become self-sufficient through successful job placement. An additional concern was the stability of the job placement: Did the clients keep their jobs once they were hired, and did their employers consider them good employees?

The evaluation of the program included the follow-up of all sixty participants one year after they left the program. There were also interviews with the employer of each participant. The results indicated that 57 percent of the participants were employed at the same job after one year, 22 percent had been promoted, and 21 percent had left the firm within three months of accepting the job. The employers of the 21 percent who left within three months commented that these women seemed to have inadequate child-care arrangements and missed work frequently because of sick children.

Based on the results of the study, the evaluator recommended that the Displaced Homemaker Center implement a day-care program, including provisions for the care of mildly ill children. The evaluator went further to comment that the success rate of the center's graduates would significantly rise if these facilities were available.

The director of the Displaced Homemaker Center investigated the cost of this recommendation and found it to be prohibitive. However, it was decided to survey existing day-care centers and to help the clients find suitable care for their young children. Thus, even though the recommendation was based on data and made sense in terms of the needs of the client group, the cost of implementing the recommendation was deemed prohibitive. However, the recommendation was not totally ignored; the center conducted the day-care survey and provided assistance in locating suitable child-care for those requesting it.

DECISION MAKING

As we've mentioned several times throughout the book, a very important component of the evaluation process is making the decision. Therefore, we've included a brief discussion of the essential steps in the decision-making process.

The value of the e-*valu*-ation and usefulness may be greatly enhanced if the steps in the decision-making process are given careful attention. Questions such as the following should be addressed:

• If several alternative recommendations are made, how do you select from among the alternatives?

• If the recommendations seem incomplete, is there anything that can be done about it?

In other words, do you, as a program manager and/or consumer of the results of an evaluation, have an opportunity to help in deciding what changes will take place, and when?

The program manager, or the person responsible for making the changes, should have a role in the formulation of the recommendations. Ideally, the list of recommendations should represent a collaborative team effort of all those participating in the evaluation process. The potential utility of the various recommendations is influenced to a large extent by the amount of understanding of all the program elements, including the clients for whom the program was designed, the deliverers of the program (teachers, counselors, nurses, social workers, and so forth), the sponsors of the program, and the community as a whole. Recommendations reflecting these understandings will probably be more useful, and have a greater probability of being implemented.

There are several stages in the decision-making process that should occur before the recommendations are made and implemented. The results (data) from the evaluation usually provide the input for this process . . . and should be used as that: data for decision making. Don't let the data dictate the decisions.

• DEFINE THE DECISIONS TO BE MADE

What, exactly, are the decisions? What do they involve? Programs? People? Resources? Knowing the types of decision to be made will facilitate the decision-making process.

• IDENTIFY THE POSSIBLE ALTERNATIVES

For each decision to be made, identify as many alternatives as possible. Be creative here, and get input from as many people as possible. Some of the alternatives might not seem reasonable; but list as many as you can and suspend your judgment about reasonableness until later.

• EXAMINE THE PROBABLE RESULTS OF EACH ALTERNATIVE

For each alternative, consider what could happen if that alternative were adopted. The potential results should be discussed with those involved with the program as well as those who will implement the recommendations.

• EVALUATE AND RANK THE ALTERNATIVES

Only after the potential impact of each alternative is carefully spelled out in terms of costs and benefits can they be evaluated and ranked. Ranking the alternatives without complete information is tantamount to ignoring much of the data gathered during the evaluation process.

• SELECT AN ALTERNATIVE

Often several alternative recommendations will be made, and the program manager or project director must decide which of these alternatives is "best" for the program, given the available resources. How, then, is the selection done? There is no correct or right way. Every situation is unique, and the choice of alternatives must reflect, first and foremost, a concern with the overall effectiveness of the program. Will the changes proposed make the program work better? Cost less? Reach a wider variety of clients? You must consider the potential impact of each alternative before deciding among them and making a recommendation for action. The decision may be that "no change" is the best choice. That's fine. If all the alternatives have been carefully considered, and the no-change option seems to be best, fine. But you must consider each alternative individually.

If the decision is made to change the program or the procedures in some way, the challenge to the manager or project director is to gain the cooperation of all those involved in the program so that the changes can be made smoothly. There are several strategies for changing behavior and gaining the cooperation of participants. We've listed some resources for you at the end of the chapter.

The decision-making process includes the selection of alternatives based on the anticipated value or impact of implementing that alternative. "No change" is also a viable alternative—as long as other possibilities are also considered.

• IMPLEMENT THE RECOMMENDATIONS

The next step in the evaluation process is the implementation of the recommendations and gaining the cooperation of the project staff and other participants. There are several factors that impede the effective use of the results of an evaluation in making valuable and important programmatic changes. One of the most important factors is communication. Inadequate communication can bring about misunderstandings concerning the reasons for making changes—or perhaps *not* making changes. A good way to obtain cooperation in the implementation process is to help people understand the *reasons* for the recommended actions.

If possible, involve those impacted in the identification of the problem, the alternatives, and the selection and implementation of the recommended solution.

• ASSESS THE RESULTS OF THE ACTION

Once the recommendations are implemented, don't stop there. Determine what happened through an evaluation similar to the one you just did. Know what you're doing and where you're going program wise, and be comfortable in the knowledge that you are filling the identified gaps in a valuable and useful manner.

SUMMARY

Reading, understanding, and acting upon the results of the evaluation are equally important components to the evaluation process as the ones we discussed earlier. To stop before the action/change occurs as a result of the evaluation, is to stop before the job is finished.

An evaluation report should contain enough information so the reader or user will know why the particular problem was selected for study, what the purpose of the evaluation was, whether the evaluators seem to have accomplished the purpose, and what specific recommendations were made on the basis of the evaluation. Involving the team members in the decison-making process is a good way to obtain their cooperation in the implementation phase. It is good to have others help specify the recommendations and consider the implications of these actions.

KEY POINTS

- An evaluation report should be clear, concise, and understandable for the intended audience.
- The report should communicate the purpose of the evaluation, whether the purpose seemed to be met, and the specific recommendations made based on the results of the evaluation.
- Although recommendations based on the data may be included in the report, decisions must be made about the usefulness of the results by those involved in the program.
- One good way to increase the chances of the recom-

mendations "working" is to use the several steps of the decison-making process:
- define the decisions to be made
- identify the possible alternatives
- examine the probable outcomes of each alternative
- evaluate and rank the alternatives
- implement the recommendations
- assess the results of the action

- Know what you're doing and where you're going (program-wise).

Selected References

1. Dichter, E. *Motivating Human Behavior*. New York: McGraw-Hill, 1971.
2. Horland, C. I., and Weiss, W. "The Influence of Source Credibility on Communication Effectiveness." *Public Opinion Quarterly* 15 (1951):635—650.
3. Janis, I. L., and Gilmore, J. B. "The Influence of Incentive Conditions on the Success of Role Playing in Modifying Attitudes." *Journal of Personality and Social Psychology* 1 (1965): 17—27.
4. Janis, I. L., and Mann, L. "A Conflict-theory Approach to Attitude Change and Decision-making." In *Psychological Foundations of Attitudes*, edited by A.G. Greenwald, et al. New York: Academic Press, 1968.
5. Lippitt, R., Watson, J., and Westley, B. *Planned Change: A Comparative Study of Principles and Techniques*. New York: Harcourt Brace Jovanovich, 1958.
6. Mann, D. "Making Change Happen?" *Teachers College Record* 77 (1976):312—322.
7. Zimbardo, P.G., Weisenberg, M., Firestone, I., and Levy, B. "Communicator Effectiveness in Producing Public Conformity and Private Attitude Change." *Journal of Personality* 33 (1965):233—256.

10
EVALUATION REVISITED —AN OVERVIEW

Identifying gaps, specifying needs, identifying goals, and objectives, finding out how well we are filling the gaps, and making recommendations for change—that's what we've been talking about throughout this book. We have attempted to demonstrate the value of knowing where you are, where you want to be, and how to identify the obstacles standing in your way. If you feel that the whole evaluation process is a valued approach to making a difference, we have succeeded. Let's review some important points, beginning with the question: Why evaluate?

Why evaluate? The many tasks and processes specified throughout this book may seem like a lot of work, but there are many good reasons to conduct an evaluation. The purposes (and reasons) for an evaluation may vary from a desire to document what is happening to a mandated requirement on the part of the funding agent. However, despite the variety of purposes, the overall goal of the evaluation process is to determine the worth or value of an organization, a program, a technique, a method of doing something, or whatever is being evaluated.

A key to achieving a useful evaluation is *action*. Thus, one important function of an evaluator is to provide information for useful decision making and subsequent action. The recommendations made, however, must make sense and be meaningful to the program manager and others who are involved in program development activities.

As a review of the evaluation process, let's start with needs assessments again.

NEEDS ASSESSMENTS

- Where are you or the program going?
- Where should you be going?
- Where are you now?
- How do you know you're going in the right direction to get where you want to be?

Doing a needs assessment can help you make sure of where you are going and can help justify the appropriateness of that direction. A need shows the polar positions of *what is* and *what should be*. The discrepancy between these two points is termed a *gap*.

Once we have identified the gaps, we should place them in priority order, selecting gaps of the highest priority for resolution. We suggest two basic types of needs assessments: external and internal. The external variety looks at gaps in outcomes, while the internal variety seeks to identify gaps in inputs, process, products, or outputs.

No matter which mode of needs assessment you select, you should come up with a list of gaps, which you then rank in order of priority. Once the gaps are in priority order, you are ready for the next step: further planning and goal setting.

PLANNING AND GOAL SETTING

Planning is used when you want to get from where you are to someplace else. Good planning involves forethought, involvement of the others in the evaluation process, and a step-by-step plan that considers where you are now, where you want to be, and how you are going to get there. Vital to the planning process are such questions as: What do I want to know as a result of this evalution? For whom is the evaluation intended? Did the program meet its intended goals?

A plan should provide a road map with specific directions and instructions as to what happens when, and who is responsible for what. It is not enough to say that you are going to evaluate a program, even if you specify which evaluation model you will be using. Much more detail is necessary. You must begin at the beginning: Why are you doing the evaluation? What specific requirement prompted this evaluation? Who, specifically, will be the consumer of the information provided by the evaluation, and how will they use the data?

Good planning includes the identification of the problem based on needs (as identified in the needs assessment). Usually the results of the needs assessment are given priorities, and the most important ones are selected for study and resolution. Once the needs (gaps) have been selected for study, we can begin to work on the detailed requirements for determining the specific kinds of information necessary to address each gap. Often it is useful to put the information in a list such as this:

Gap Identified	Data Required	Availability of Data
1.		
2.		
3.		
(etc.)		

Will data have to be collected specifically for this evaluation, or are data available from existing sources? Are the instruments readily available, or will they have to be designed? What scale of measurement is used on the various instruments?

Planning also involves the selection of an evaluation model, or a portion of a model, that best fits our purposes. Where in the whole organizational elements model did we begin? What models are most appropriate to allow the kinds of decisions we want to make?

Planning also includes specification of hypotheses as well as selection of statistical tests. Careful thought and consideration of the kinds of decisions you want to make will help ensure that you collect the "right" data to make those decisions.

Thus, good planning begins before an evaluation and gives direction to the entire process. A clear and concise road map will help communicate to others what you are up to and will help keep you on the right track. A good plan will specify both a beginning and an end for the evaluation, so that you not only know where to begin, but also know when you have finished. The better the planning, the greater the chance that your evaluation will be a success and will allow you to make the kinds of decisions you want to make.

Goals and objectives are statements of intended results that are measurable. Goals are usually more general and are often measured on the nominal or ordinal level: Were we successful? Did the children learn to read? Do they feel better about themselves now? Objectives are usually more specific and are measured on the interval or ratio level. Both are important in evaluation.

Because of their greater specificity, objectives are often found to be more useful in identifying and defining the intended program results. A list of specific objectives will state exactly what you expect the program to accomplish. It will also help identify the type of data required to determine whether a particular objective has been met.

EVALUATION MODELS

We mentioned several evaluation models that are useful in diverse situations as well as for various elements of the organizational model. You do not have to adopt a model in its entirety; you can be eclectic and select those aspects that will provide the answers to the questions you've asked. But you must be aware that there is a diversity of models from which to choose so that you can make the best choice for your purposes.

Here, briefly, is a review of the eight models we discussed. There are two major types: goal-based and goal-free. If you still have questions go back to Chapter 6 and/or read some of the references suggested at the end of that chapter.

Scriven's Formative-Summative model is concerned with both the worth of the goals and the extent to which the goals have been met. Formative evaluation involves the assessment of the gaps in process while summative evaluation deals with assessing the status of the gaps after the completion of the program.

The emphasis in the CIPP model is on the provision of information for decision makers other than the evaluator; thus a team effort is necessary. Data for decisions are collected during the planning (context), structuring (input), implementing (process), and recycling (product) phases. (Remember that these terms—*input* and *process*—differ in usage in the CIPP model and in our organizational elements model.) However, you may choose to do a less than complete evaluation after the planning stage has been completed. In this case, you could use a portion of this model.

The CSE-UCLA model emphasizes the provision of information for decision makers; it would be useful in situations similar to those where the CIPP model could be used. The one difference between the models is that the CSE model allows you to evaluate both the implementation *process* and the in-process (en-route) *products*.

Stake's Countenance model adds an emphasis on gathering data to describe the events of the planning/implementation/outcome phases as well as the provision of data for the decision-making or *judgment process*. In addition, one must be able to specify the standards used for judging the program.

Tyler's Goal Attainment model emphasizes the specification of goals and the determination of the extent to which the goals have been attained. Each goal is transcribed into a behavioral objective that is measurable; thus this model emphasizes measurement and the quantifying of behavior.

Provus' Discrepancy model focuses on discrepancies between the standards that have been set and the actual performance. When discrepancies are noted, the decision must be made as to whether to change the standards or to modify the program in some way so that the performance is changed. The discrepancies are identified and dealt with throughout the entire program development process, beginning with the installation phase and continuing through a cost-benefit analysis at the end of the program.

The above models are goal-based in that they work with the goals as specified by the program developers and judge the program results in terms of these goals.

Scriven's Goal-Free Evaluation model looks at the actual results of the program, whether planned or unplanned. The premise of goal-free evaluation is that by not limiting oneself to the stated goals, the evaluator can be more open to the total impact, both positive and negative, of the program. Goal-free evaluation is not really free of all goals, only of producer or program goals. Thus, this model is useful for identifying serendipitous occurrences, which may be overlooked with the goal-based models.

Goal-free evaluation can be used in conjunction with any of the goal-based models. By combining the two, you can identify both intended and unintended results.

Stake's Responsive Evaluation model emphasizes the natural communication of the results rather than a formal written report. In addition, data are collected through interviews with clients, audiences—anyone who might be impacted in some way by the program. A thorough description of the on-going program activities is also part of the data collected, and the evaluator often acts as a participant-observer. Responsive evaluation is particularly useful for art, music, and other humanities programs.

Which model is best for your purposes? It depends on the questions you want to address and the aspects of the program you want to evaluate. The ideal situation is one in which you are involved in the initial planning phases and can incorporate the evaluation plan into the whole of the program development process.

TOOLS OF EVALUATION

The tools of evaluation include a variety of statistical techniques suitable for various situations. Ask yourself the following questions and use the Decision Maps provided in Chapter 7 to be reasonably sure that your choice is correct:

- What level of data do you have? (nominal, ordinal, interval, ratio)
- What do you want to know? (description, differences, relationship)
- How many groups of subjects are you working with? (one group, one group with pre- and post-measures, two groups)

Statistical significance is a probability statement reflecting how sure you are that the observed results are really happening and not just a chance occurrence. Since it is only a probability statement, by itself it isn't very meaningful. The importance of the results may have little to do with the statistical significance.

Practical importance is a value judgment on the part of the researcher. What do the results mean in terms of the overall evaluation? The informed judgment of the researcher as to what the results mean is a most important result of the analysis. Statistical results, by themselves, are simply groups of numbers. A person must attach meaning to these numbers.

MAKING DECISIONS AND RECOMMENDATIONS

A very important part of the evaluation process is making the decisions and recommendations that will bring about planned and constructive change. In making the decisions, go back to the beginning, to the needs assessment and the gaps that were identified. The decisions and recommendations should directly reflect these gaps. Be sure you understand what's gone on so that you can communicate it to others and so that it is understandable to those who will use the results of your evaluation.

The clarity of the final written report of the evaluation is very important. Not only is it important in documenting the evaluation process, but it is also useful in gaining the cooperation of those who will implement the recommended changes. The changes being recommended are based on data; the means you used to identify, collect, analyze, and interpret the data should not be a secret. Gaining cooperation in program improvement is crucial. A manager or administrator cannot impose changes on an organization and expect such changes to be readily accepted. To facilitate behavior change as well as program change, those involved in implementing the changes must be convinced of the worth of these activities.

WHAT DO YOU PLAN TO DO NOW?

Well, here you are near the end of this book. What effect has your reading had on future decisions? What do you plan to do differently now? These questions are the bottom line of the effect of our book on you. Let's summarize some of the ideas and attitudes that were the intention of this book.

First, a few *don'ts:*

1. *Don't be afraid of evaluation.* We see evaluation as a valuable tool to help identify gaps, set goals, formulate

objectives, measure behaviors, and determine exactly how you and your program are faring in filling the gaps. We hope we've helped you to see how valuable evaluation can be, and we hope we have given you enough help through our examples so that you're not afraid to try it.

2. *Don't be overwhelmed by data.* Use them as they are—instances of measurable program outcomes. Sometimes beginning evaluators feel that they can't see the forest for the trees, can't make sense out of the data because of their sheer volume. If this happens to you, stop. Match the data with your objectives, and match your objectives to the organizational elements. See where each set of scores belongs (which gap it addresses). Any new venture can seem over-powering. If you concentrate on one step at a time, you probably won't get "data snowed."

3. *Don't assume you know all about the programs.* Use partners in helping to identify gaps, in specifying goals and objectives, in all phases of the evaluation process. Another good reason to find partners is that those actively involved in the evaluation process are more likely to accept the changes recommended and to facilitate their implementation.

4. *Don't be afraid of statistics.* We realize that the mere mention of the word sets many knees to trembling, but by using the Decision Maps in Chapter 7, you will be able to identify the appropriate statistical tests for your purposes. Avoid overly sophisticated and complex techniques that you don't understand. It's extremely difficult to make *sensible* conclusions and recommendations on the basis of analyses you don't understand.

Now for a few *dos:*

1. *Do plan evaluation.* Involve others in the planning and encourage their commitment.

2. *Do establish goals.* How can you know where you're going without a designated end point or goal? Don't set goals by yourself. Get help, especially from those who will benefit from the results of the evaluation.

3. *Do use results in making change*. Why bother doing an evaluation if it's not going to have an impact on the system?

4. *Do involve others*. Partners ease the pain and make more time available for you to do other things. They are helpful in identifying available resources and in doing many of the tasks of evaluation.

5. *Do use the tools appropriate to your data collection and reporting plan*. Using the Decision Maps in Chapter 7 and the computation guides in the Appendix and other resources such as statistics books, you will be able to make an informed decision—and even understand what you've doing well enough to explain it to others!

6. *Do see evaluation as a continuing process*, not just a one-shot activity. Plan evaluation early and incorporate it into all phases of your program.

7. *Do have faith in knowing where you are,* where you are going, and how you're going to get there.

A SIMPLIFIED EVALUATION PROCEDURE

We have covered what an evaluation does and some of the considerations and procedures for implementing a successful evaluation.

This is a final review, and presents the functions and the order of doing the functions for developing and conducting an evaluation.

Each of the functions which have to be performed are presented—follow the solid lines and arrows along the pathway. Under each function is listed the page on which the content and procedures of that function are presented.

You might use this flow chart as a guide in planning and conducting an evaluation. Remember, this is a simple guide. You should draw up your own evaluation plan using some of the techniques and procedures presented in Chapter 4.

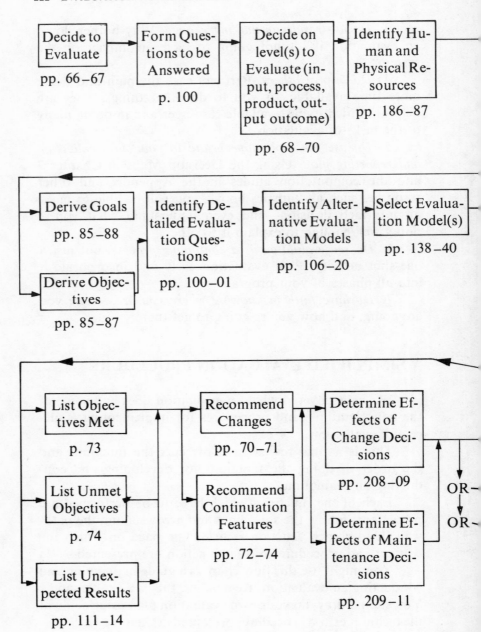

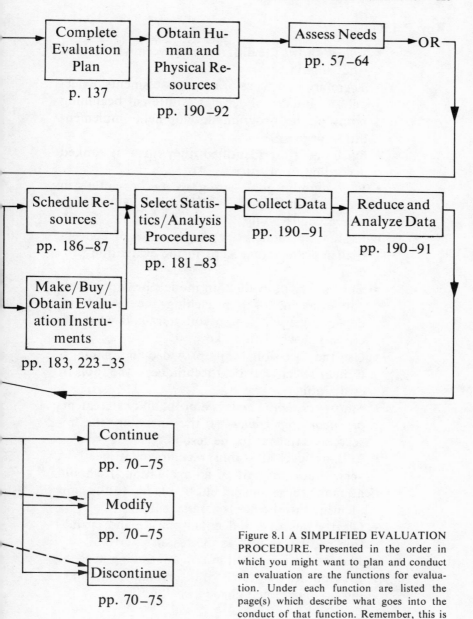

Figure 8.1 A SIMPLIFIED EVALUATION PROCEDURE. Presented in the order in which you might want to plan and conduct an evaluation are the functions for evaluation. Under each function are listed the page(s) which describe what goes into the conduct of that function. Remember, this is a general guide only.

Key Points

- A *need* shows the difference between what is and what should be.
- There are two types of needs assessments: external and internal. Each has a different beginning point in the program/development implementation process.
- Once needs are identified, they must be ranked according to priority.
- Planning and goal setting are two essentials in the evaluation process. They help you define where you're going.
- Evaluation models are simply ways of conceptualizing the actual steps in the evaluation process.
- The variety of evaluation models provides alternative means of approaching the evaluation, depending upon where you start and what decision you want to make.
- Use the Decision Maps provided in Chapter 7 to help select statistical techniques—the tools of evaluation.
- *Statistical significance* is a probability statement; *practical importance* is the meaning the researcher attaches to the results.
- Making decisions and recommendations is a very important part of an evaluation. It should all make sense and should be related to the gaps identified in the needs assessment.
- Clearly describe and communicate the evaluation process as well as the results.
- Plan and use evaluation as a continuing process.
- Incorporate the results of the evaluation in making organizational change.

APPENDIX
INSTRUMENTATION

Selecting or devising an instrument to collect the data for your evaluation is one of the most important steps in the whole evaluation process. Even if your program is effective and is doing exactly what it's supposed to do, you may not be able to tell this if you use inappropriate instruments to collect the data. In this Appendix we will discuss the most important aspects of selecting an instrument and then describe some of the basic considerations in writing your own instrument. There are many excellent books on testing and measurement, some of which are included in the reference list at the end of this Appendix. It probably would be a good idea to check these sources as well.

SELECTING AN INSTRUMENT

There are many things to think about when selecting an instrument to measure the impact of some aspect of a program. First, what type of instrument will you require? An achievement test? An aptitude measure? An attitude, opinion, or interest scale? There is a variety of types of measures, many of which are described in *Buros's Mental Measurements Yearbooks*. Second, how do you know the test is measuring what it's supposed to, that it's valid and reliable? Third, what about the practical considerations: cost, ease of administering and scoring, and availability? In the next few pages, we'll give you some information to help you answer some of these questions so that you can work with a testing specialist and be sure you're getting what you want.

TYPES OF TESTS

There are many ways to classify tests, but we are going to limit the discussion here to some types that are more commonly used for evaluation: achievement tests, where one is interested in determining whether certain ideas, skills, or materials have been mastered; personality measures such as self-concept, adjustment, sociability, preferences, and so forth, which may be useful in evaluating various aspects of a program; and measures of typical performance, including attitude, opinion, and interest scales. We'll describe each of these three kinds of tests and suggest some sources of further information.

ACHIEVEMENT TESTS

The achievement test is useful if you want to determine whether the clients participating in your program have mastered certain concepts or materials. Achievement tests are usually administered both before and after a program, and any differences (hopefully gains) between the before and after scores are attributed to the program. In selecting an achievement test, you must be sure the test actually measures what is being taught in the program. For example, if you selected a numerical ability test that stressed computations, while the program you are planning to evaluate teaches concepts and understandings related to numerical ability, it is quite likely that a pretest—post-test would not show much difference because the test is measuring one aspect of numerical ability and the program is teaching another. You must be sure the achievement test you select really is measuring the same skills that the program is teaching.

Another question to ask yourself in selecting an achievement test is: Do I want norm-referenced or criterion-referenced information? We mentioned the pretest—post-test comparisons above, but this type of comparison does not preclude making other types of comparisons in order to determine how the clients compare to other standards. A criterion-referenced test means that some standard or criterion has been set by the test developers, and the information yielded by the test allows you to make comparisons to see how well the clients are doing as compared to some preset performance standard.

Criterion-referenced tests are particularly useful when you are interested in determining the point at which clients have reached an established level of performance. A person's performance on the test is not compared to that of any other person, only to the preset standard or criterion. In addition, criterion-referenced tests are not designed to discriminate among clients; usually little variability in scores is evidenced. The emphasis is on what a person knows, *not* how much one knows as compared to someone else.

Another term used in relation to an achievement test is *norm-referenced*. A norm-referenced test is designed to provide information about a person's performance as compared to the performance of a norm or comparison group. It does not necessarily provide information as to the amount of material the person has mastered. Scores on norm-referenced tests are thus interpreted in terms of comparing a person's performance to a group. For example, a score of 20 may indicate that the person earning this score surpassed 90 percent of the norm group (that would be good), or it may indicate that the person surpassed only 5 percent of the norm group (that would be bad).

You would have to check the score with "norm" tables to determine exactly what a given score meant. A norm-referenced test gives information about how well a person performed on the test as compared to the norm group; it does not give any information in terms of the amount of knowledge the person has, only how that person's score compares with those of a group.

The test manual, designed by the test publisher to provide a variety of information about the test, may provide information about several norm groups. Since this is usually the case, it is important to select the norm group whose characteristics most closely resemble those of the client group you're working with. With each table giving the norm data, there will be a description of the people in the norm group. It is very important to select an appropriate norm or comparison group. For example, suppose that your client group is made up of returning women who are not college graduates. If you use college graduates as a norm or comparison group, your clients may look like low achievers simply because you selected an inappropriate comparison group. Therefore, when choosing a norm-referenced test, you must pay particular attention to the characteristics of the norm group in addition to the other considerations discussed below.

However, as with the criterion-referenced tests, you may use the norm-referenced test as pretest—post-test measures and not use the comparisons with the norm group. By doing so, however, you would be ignoring potentially valuable information about how your clients were performing in comparison to some other group. The norm-comparison data may give you information about how well your clients are performing as compared with some segment of society, and they may provide information about whether your clients will be able to function—and be self-sufficient—in society.

PERSONALITY MEASURES

Measures of personality aren't really tests (they don't have correct answers), but they do provide indications of a person's thinking or feeling about aspects of self or about some object or topic. There is a variety of personality measures. Some deal with a relatively narrowly defined construct, such as sociability. Others are more general and provide information about several aspects of personality. Many of the items on the personality tests are quite personal, and the respondent is expected to reveal aspects of self and inner feelings. Some respondents may feel uncomfortable with measures such as these, and their responses may not reflect their true feelings and ideas. Thus it is extremely important to gain the cooperation of the clients so that the data accurately reflect what's really happening.

If you do decide to include some type of personality measure in your evaluation plan, it would be a good idea to check the instrument carefully to be sure it will give you the type of information you want and that it will not be considered offensive by your client group. Personality measures are used less often than achievement tests and should be used only when those involved with presenting and using the results of the evaluation understand the limitations of these types of measures.

TESTS OF TYPICAL PERFORMANCE

Included in this category are measures of attitudes, opinions, interests, and so forth. These types of measures, although less frequently used in evaluations than achievement tests, may be useful in providing information about the affective impact of the program. As with achievement tests, they may be used in pretest and post-test situations to detect whether any changes have taken place. Although observed changes in these variables may or may not have come about because of the program, careful designing of the questions and data collection should provide some valuable information about how the clients or the community feel about the program, the ideas contained within the program, or other related aspects.

CONSIDERATIONS IN SELECTING TESTS

There are two broad and important considerations in choosing an instrument: the psychometric and the practical. The psychometric concerns include reliability (Is the test measuring consistently whatever it is measuring?) and validity (Is the test really measuring whatever it is supposed to be measuring?). The practical concerns include cost; ease of administration, scoring, and interpretation; availability of testing materials; and similar considerations. Although the psychometric concerns should be paramount, you should not ignore the practical considerations either. Some tests should only be given and interpreted by trained specialists (such as school psychologists).

RELIABILITY

Whether the test measures the behavior consistently is the concern of reliability.

In general, the longer the test, the more reliable it is because it gives a more representative sample of the person's behavior. However, if the test is excessively long, a person may become tired, bored, or frustrated and not do well on the test. In such cases the test would not be representative of the person's knowledge, feelings, beliefs, and so on. Therefore, test developers try to strike a happy medium—long enough to get a good picture of the person's behavior, but not so long as to bore or tire the person.

There are several types of reliability, and each is reported as a correlation coefficient, ranging from 0 to 1.0 (no negatives here). The various types of reliability are appropriate in different situations, so be sure to determine whether the appropriate type of reliability coefficient is reported. The three most commonly used types of reliability are: 1) stability, 2) equivalence, and 3) internal consistency.

STABILITY

One type of reliability has to do with how *stable* the measurement is over time and is usually reported as test-retest reliability. Here the instrument is administered to the same group of people at two different times, which may be days, weeks, or months apart. The results from the two administrations are correlated, and the higher the coefficient, the more consistently the behavior is measured over time. A coefficient of stability, as this type of reliability is sometimes called, is particularly important in pretest—posttest situations. You would be concerned with whether the behavior is measured consistently over time so that any changes noted may be attributed to program effects rather than fluctuations in measurement.

EQUIVALENCE

A type of reliability concerned with whether two forms of a test are consistently measuring the same behavior is called the *coefficient of equivalence*. Sometimes the two forms of a test are called "parallel forms" or "alternate forms." To determine the coefficient of equivalence, the two forms of the test are administered to a group of people at the same time, or a very short time apart. The results are then correlated, and the higher the correlation, the more consistently the two forms of the test are measuring the behavior.

The coefficient of equivalence is especially important in a pretest—posttest situation when the test questions are unique and the clients might remember items. This may be the case with problem-solving tests—once a person has solved the problem, even if the test is administered again six months later, it may be easy to remember the answer, so the second administration of the test is not so much a test of problem-solving skills as of memory. If you administer a test only once, at the end of the program, then either the coefficient of stability or equivalence will be useful information.

INTERNAL CONSISTENCY

The type of reliability concerned with whether the test is consistently measuring the behavior throughout the entire test is called the *coefficient of internal consistency*. This type of reliability is often reported as *split half*, where one half of the test is correlated with the other half, or as a formula such as KR 20, KR 21, or coefficient *alpha*. The coefficient *alpha* is a generalized form of the KR formulas developed specifically for personality measures where there is no "right" answer. Coefficients of internal consistency are not appropriate with speed tests or tests with specific time limits. When a person takes a timed test and stops to work on a difficult item, several items may be missed that could have been answered had sufficient time been given.

Note that throughout our discussion of reliability we have been concerned only with the consistency with which *some behavior* is being measured. Note that we don't know *what* behavior is being measured—only that some behavior is being measured consistently. *What* is actually being measured is the concern of validity.

VALIDITY

The extent to which a test is really measuring what it purports to measure is indicated by the validity of the test. There are four types of validity; each is appropriate in different circumstances and for different types of tests. Rarely, if ever, would you be concerned with all four types of validity for one particular instrument.

CONTENT VALIDITY

Content validity is primarily concerned with the content of the test. Does it represent the behavior domain it purports to represent? This type of validity is particularly important for an achievement test. Does the test you select really measure the content taught in the program? Content validity may be determined by a panel of experts who determine if the test appears to be measuring what it says it is. A method of establishing content validity is through a table of specifications where different areas of achievement are specified and the test is evaluated against this table to determine how thoroughly the content area has been covered. Content validity is seldom reported empirically; instead, a description is given of how it was done, and a general statement is made about the outcome.

PREDICTIVE VALIDITY

Predictive validity is one of two types of criterion validities and has to do with how well the test predicts some carefully specified behavior or results. Predictive validity is particularly important in any test used for selection or screening purposes. Predictive validity is usually reported as a correlation coefficient—between the test and the results it is supposed to predict. In looking at the predictive validity of a test, it is very important to look at what is being predicted and to determine if this is the behavior you are interested in predicting. For example, if a "successful job behavior" test was validated against the criterion of obtaining a job and you were interested in predicting whether the person would be successful in keeping the job for at least six months, then the reported validity coefficient doesn't tell you much since you are interested in predicting a different result. The test may or may not work, but either way the predictive validity coefficient given doesn't provide the type of information you require.

In choosing a test to predict behavior or another result, pay particular attention to the criterion used in establishing predictive validity and decide whether that criterion is important and useful to you for your purposes.

CONCURRENT VALIDITY

Concurrent validity is the second type of criterion validity. The most common use of concurrent validity is in the development of objective, pencil-and-paper tests to measure behaviors that are usually measured by interviews, clinical judgments, or individual testing situations. The validity coefficient here reflects the degree of relationship between the shorter, pencil-and-paper test and the longer, interview situation. Note that the assumption is made that the longer, individual form of the test is valid—that it really measures what it says it does.

Concurrent validity would be of interest when a pencil-and-paper test is used to replace clinical judgment, such as in a job interview situation.

CONSTRUCT VALIDITY

Construct validity is the most difficult type of validity to establish; yet it is the most important for instruments such as personality measures and attitude scales. Construct validity addresses this question: "To what extent is the underlying construct, as defined by the personality variable, really measured by the test?"

Because most personality variables, such as self-concept, sociability, and dependence, are difficult constructs to define, it follows that establishing the validity of these tests would also be difficult. One of the best methods of establishing construct validity is the multitrait, multimethod technique developed by Campbell and Fiske. The details of this technique are beyond the scope of the present discussion; however, if you are using any type of personality measure in your evaluation, be sure that construct validity has been adequately established.

Validity is a more important concern than reliability. A test can be reliable but not valid; the reverse is not true. Since the central concern of validity is "truth," or the extent to which a test really measures what it purports to measure, validity is of crucial importance in selecting tests to measure the effectiveness of your program.

PRACTICAL CONSIDERATIONS

Although the psychometric properties of reliability and validity are essential for any test, other things being equal, there are some practical considerations also. The first of these is *cost*—both of the testing materials and the scoring. For example, some tests can be purchased only if they are scored by the firm selling the tests. The need to purchase the scoring each time the tests are used may limit the utility of the test. Therefore, in selecting a test, consider the initial cost of the materials, the cost of scoring the results (by the company selling the tests or by one of your staff members), and the probable (or possible) reuse of the materials in the future.

A second practical consideration is *ease of administration*. Will the person giving the test require special training? Can a large group of people be tested at one time? Are the instructions clearly presented so that they are easily understood by those who will administer the test?

A third consideration is *time*. How long will it take to administer the various instruments you've selected? Will it be necessary to administer the tests at more than one sitting? If you have selected several tests that will take more than a total of sixty minutes to administer, then more than one session is probably desirable. Is this possible? Will you, or the project manager, be able to schedule this much time?

Another consideration is the availability of *parallel forms* of a test. If you decide that parallel forms of a test are necessary, you will then be limited to those tests for which the two or more forms are available.

The type of information provided by the *test manual* is another practical consideration. If you are interested in comparing your clients with a norm group, are the norm groups appropriate? There may be several tests that are quite similar in several respects, but different in the type of norm data available. As noted earlier, inappropriate norm groups may yield invalid comparisons—and your program will not be given a fair evaluation.

One last point on practical considerations. Be sure the *reading level* and *content level* are appropriate. A test that cannot be understood will obviously not give accurate information.

In summary, then, in choosing a test devised by professional psychometricians, the psychometric concerns of validity and reliability come first, followed by the practical considerations discussed above. Instead of selecting a test published by a reputable publisher, you may select a "research form" of a test that is under development. If you do this, be sure to look carefully at the validity and reliability and whatever other data are available. If you have carefully and thoroughly examined all sources of published tests and measurements and still have not found anything suitable, you may have to resort to devising your own test. However, we urge you to look *very* carefully before doing this because the construction of any test requires the establishment of the reliability and validity of that measure—a task that can be costly and time-consuming.

DESIGNING A TEST

If, after a careful and thorough search, you determine there are no appropriate instruments to use in your evaluation, then you might consider either writing an instrument specifically for your evaluation project, or hiring a consultant to do the task for you. Achievement tests are less difficult to construct than the other types discussed earlier, but any test construction is a difficult, time-consuming, and challenging process. We strongly recommend that you do not attempt to devise any type of test or instrument other than an achievement test; therefore, the information presented below will be limited to those issues relevant to achievement test construction.

PLANNING THE TEST

A good achievement test is the result of careful planning; it doesn't just happen by itself. The test must reflect the content of the program or curriculum—in other words it must have *content validity*. One way to be sure the test does in fact cover the material taught is to use a table of specifications. This table, or chart, can be used as a guide to ensure that all content areas are adequately covered. The table is usually two-dimensional and specifies the content as well as the types of behaviors the client should be able to display. There are several useful taxonomies of behavior. One is Bloom's, which includes knowing, comprehending, applying, analyzing, synthesizing, and evaluating. Thus, the program developer must be able to specify the types of behaviors the clients will possess after completion of the program as well as the types of content. An example of a table of specifications is presented below.

BEHAVIORS

	Knowing	Compre-hending	Applying	Analyz-ing	Synthe-sizing	Evaluat-ing
C 1*						
O						
N 2						
T						
E 3						
N						
T 4						

*Each numbered line refers to a different content area; this example matrix would contain four different content areas.

The cells of the table are used to indicate the number of questions on the test that reflect a certain content area and a particular level of behavior. This way the test developer can be certain that the test accurately reflects both the variety of desired outcome behaviors and the content of the program.

A test developer is not limited to the behaviors specified in a taxonomy. Any action verb will probably work—but these must be identified in collaboration with the program developer, and they must make sense.

If the program has been carefully planned, then probably a set of behavioral objectives has been developed. If this is the case, you will probably find them quite helpful in writing test items. Thus, the use of behavioral objectives is a second approach to devising a good achievement test. A good, clear behavioral objective could correspond to one cell in the table of specifications in that it should contain information about the content and behavior. Thus, each objective can be used to generate one or two questions for your test.

After the planning of the content for the test has been completed (a complete set of behavioral objectives or a table of specifications), you are ready to begin constructing items. What types of items will work best—short answer, essay, or closed response, such as true-false or multiple-choice? The type of item you choose will depend on your client group, the type of content to be covered on the test, and the amount of time allotted for testing.

Closed form questions (such as multiple-choice) are particularly suitable for factual material where there is one best or correct answer. More material can be covered with these types of questions since the person usually must only recall or recognize the answer rather than constructing an answer as for an essay test. Some clients perceive the closed form item as being easier to answer; it is certainly easier to score since one has only to add the number of correct responses.

The most commonly used closed form question is the multiple-choice format, in which an item stem is presented and several possible alternatives are presented. Multiple-choice questions can be used to assess a variety of behaviors (such as those in Bloom's taxonomy) as well as a wide range of content. Although good multiple-choice items are difficult to construct, they can provide the evaluator with some information on the extent to which the program content has been mastered. The multiple-choice question consists of a stem and the alternatives, which include the best or correct answer and several "distractors." The better the distractors are, the more thoroughly the clients must know the content or information if they are to select the best alternative.

The true-false item is another type of closed form question. It usually consists of a statement to which the client responds "True" or "False." At times the client is asked to change a false item in order to make it true. This type of item is particularly good for determining the extent to which particular concepts are understood. However, there are many types of content and behavior that cannot be adequately measured with a true-false item. For example, determining a client's ability to analyze or synthesize information would be quite difficult to determine with this type of question format.

The matching item is yet another type of closed form question. It has many similarities to the multiple-choice format and is useful whenever particular sets of information are interrelated. Matching items consist of a series of stems and alternatives. Good matching items have a series of alternatives that are possible for each stem so that the person has to know the material well in order to match the correct stem and alternative. Often it is best to have more alternatives than stems so that the person must rely on knowledge rather than the process of elimination.

There is no particular advantage in using matching items rather than multiple-choice or vice versa. If you want to vary the format or save space, then matching items are a possibility. Both types have the advantages of being able to cover a broad range of content in a relatively short time and of being quite easy to score. The disadvantage is that it is difficult to devise really good items.

The alternative to closed form questions is open form questions, including short answers, sentence completion, and essay. For the most part, open form questions are easier to write but more difficult to score. There is usually a value judgment involved in determining what constitutes a right answer. However, one advantage of this type of question is that it is extremely difficult to guess—the person must know the material quite well in order to write about it.

LENGTH OF THE TEST

We mentioned earlier that the longer a test is, the more reliable it is because of the more representative sample of behavior that can be obtained. However, there is an optimum length—long enough to give a good sample of behavior but short enough so that the person doesn't become overly tired or frustrated. Usually this would be about one hour of testing time—or about fifty multiple-choice questions or seventy-five true-false items. On open form questions, it would depend upon how much you're asking the person to write (completing a sentence or a one-page essay). In addition, there is more variability in the time necessary for responding to open form questions. Some people spend much time in organizing their thoughts before writing, and others simply begin to write. For the purposes of determining how much content was learned from a particular program, a one-hour multiple-choice test is probably most satisfactory.

Specific information on writing and evaluating items may be found in some of the sources listed in the reference section of this Appendix.

ETHICS OF TESTING

Administering instruments of any sort, and using the resulting scores to make decisions about programs and people, is a tremendous responsibility. One must be sure that the instruments are appropriate, that they are administered in the proper way, and that the scores are interpreted accurately. For these reasons, it is often desirable to work with a person who specializes in tests and testing—perhaps a psychometrician or school psychologist.

As we suggested in our discussion of practical considerations in choosing a test, one may pay attention to the reliability, validity, availability of norms, and reading (or difficulty) level of the test. A person trained in testing is better able to assist in the evaluation of these factors.

A second reason for working with a testing specialist is that there are prerequisites for administering and scoring the test. Most standardized achievement tests must be given under special conditions—timing, the reading of instructions, and the answering of questions by participants. It is extremely important that all testing conditions be exactly as specified in the test manual. Failure to follow the instructions may result in the test being invalidated; therefore, any scores obtained would be meaningless.

Incorrect or inaccurate scoring will also bring about problems. For example, if the tests are scored by hand, care must be taken to assure that no clerical errors occur. If machine scoring is used, care must be taken not to tear, fold, or make extraneous marks on the score sheets. Failure to complete the scoring procedures as required in the test manual, may lead to erroneous data—and perhaps faulty decisions about the program.

Interpretation of test scores is an extremely sensitive area—and one that even a professional approaches with some hesitation. Test scores have been used in the past to "label" a person, that is, to suggest that one test score does in fact reflect a person's "true" nature. However, a test represents only one small sample of a person's total behavior repertoire, and to make judgments based on one small sample may lead to inappropriate conclusions.

Although care should be taken in administering the test to assure that all participants are comfortable, are able to hear the directions, and have a pencil to work with, there is no way to assure that all participants are equally alert and are not anxious about the testing situation. Thus, extreme caution should be exercised in interpreting test scores, particularly the scores of individuals.

Many instruments, especially standardized achievement tests and various personality and attitude scales, require close attention to test security. For these instruments, usually only specially trained persons are able to buy and use them. If, for example, everyone who was interested could obtain a copy of the exact Graduate Record Examination (GRE) that they are scheduled to take, the test would no longer be valid for its purpose: predicting success in graduate school. Thus, for many different instruments, test security is very important. Practice with the test would invalidate the purpose of the test.

An individual's right to privacy is yet another ethical consideration of the testing situation. When test scores are used as a part of the evaluation process, the scores of the group as a whole are usually considered, rather than the scores of an individual. When this is the case, there is often no reason for a person's name to be on the test; a number or other type of coding is often sufficient. Test data about particular individuals should never be given to anyone else without the consent of the individual being tested. For your own protection, it is usually best to have the permission in writing.

If you work with a testing specialist, and are sensitive to a person's right to privacy and confidentiality of testing information, you are most likely to have good and valid data. The use of instruments and tests is a responsibility which must be assumed by those responsible for the evaluation. Misuse and abuse of tests and test scores often have serious consequences, not the least of which may be inappropriate decisions about the impact and effectiveness of the program being evaluated.

Recent attention has been given to assure that any test or assessment vehicle and procedure is "culturally fair"— that it does not penalize an individual for coming from different cultural or learning backgrounds than another group. When giving tests, and interpreting data, make certain that there is no cultural bias in the instruments, procedures, instructions and thus, in the interpretations. Again, a testing or counseling specialist can help you assure that you are using culturally "fair" tests and procedures.

Selected References

1. Buros, O. K., ed. *Seventh Mental Measurements Yearbook*. Highland Park, N.J.: Gryphon Press, 1972.
2. Gronlund, N. W. *Preparing Criterion-referenced Tests for Classroom Use.* New York: Macmillan, 1973.
3. Hambleton, R. K., and Novick, M. R. "Toward an Integration of Theory and Method for Criterion-referenced Tests." *Journal of Educational Measurement* 10 (1973): 159–170.
4. Popham, W. J., and Husek, T. R. "Implications of Criterion-referenced Measurement." *Journal of Educational Measurement* 6 (1969): 1–9.
5. American Psychological Association. *Standards for Educational and Psychological Tests and Manuals.* Washington, D.C.: A.P.A., 1966.
6. Campbell, D. T., and Fiske, D. W. "Convergent and Discriminant Validity by the Multitrait-multimethod Matrix." *Psychological Bulletin* 65 (1959): 81–105.
7. Hills, J. R. *Measurement and Evaluation in the Classroom.* Columbus, Ohio: C. E. Merrill, 1976.
8. Bloom, B., ed. *Taxonomy of Educational Objectives: Handbook I: Cognitive Domain.* New York: McKay, 1956.
9. Mager, R. *Preparing Instructional Objectives.* 2nd ed. Belmont, Calif.: Fearon, 1975.

10. Anastasi, A. *Psychological Testing*. (4th ed.) New York: Macmillan, 1976.
11. Diener, Edward and Crandall, Rick. *Ethics in social and behavioral research*. Chicago: University of Chicago Press, 1978.
12. *Ethical Principles in the conduct of research with human participants*. Washington, D.C.: American Psychological Association, 1973.

Other Useful References

Downie, N. W. *Fundamentals of Measurement*. 2nd. ed. New York: Oxford University Press, 1967.

Ebel, R. L. *Essentials of Educational Measurement*. Englewood Cliffs, N.J.: Prentice-Hall, 1972.

Ebel, R. L. "How to Write True-False Items." *Educational and Psychological Measurement* 31 (1971): 417–426.

Educational Testing Service. *Tests and Measurement Kit*. Princeton, N. J.: Educational Testing Service, 1963.

Gronlund, N. W. *Constructing Achievement Tests*. Englewood Cliffs, N. J.: Prentice-Hall, 1968.

Schoer, L. A. *Test Construction: A Programmed Guide*. Boston: Allyn & Bacon, 1970.

Shaw, M. E., and Wright, T. *Scales for the Measurement of Attitudes*. New York: McGraw-Hill, 1967.

Thorndike, R. L., ed. *Educational Measurement*. 2nd. ed. Washington, D.C.: American Council on Education, 1971.

Webb, E. J., Campbell, D. T., Schwartz, R. D., and Sechrest, L. *Unobtrusive Measures: Nonreactive Research in the Social Sciences*. Chicago: Rand McNally, 1966.

Welch, W. W., and Walberg, H. J. "Pretest and Sensitization Effects in Curriculum Evaluation." *American Educational Research Journal* 7 (1970): 605–614.

Wood, D. A. *Test Construction: Development and Interpretation of Achievement Tests*. Columbus, Ohio: C. E. Merrill, 1960.

INDEX

ABOUT THE AUTHORS

Dr. Roger Kaufman is Professor, Department of Educational Research and Director, Center for Needs Assessment and Planning, Learning Systems Institute, Florida State University. He was previously a professor at the United States International University, Chapman College and the University of Southern California. His Ph.D. is from New York University, and he is a diplomat of the American Board of Professional Psychology and a Fellow of the American Psychological Association. He has written a number of books in planning, needs assessment, and organizational behavior, and has authored over fifty professional articles in needs assessment, planning, and evaluation, as well as in organizational development and policy. He has served as a consultant to numerous public agencies, ranging from the Secretary of Health, Education and Welfare, the Secretary of the Navy, various school systems, medical and nursing schools, and industrial organizations.

Dr. Susan Thomas, whose Ph.D. is from Purdue University, is an Associate Professor, Department of Home and Family Life, College of Home Economics at Florida State University. There, she teaches graduate courses in testing and research design; she was previously on the faculty of the University of Illinois. She is also Director of the Resource Center for Women's Programs; the Center provides training and technical assistance in program development and evaluation. She is also study director of major research projects on women in society and on human services delivery systems; author of articles on statistics, measurement and testing; and a consultant and lecturer on evaluation.

DATE DUE

ILL 7-2185			
11-26-76			
3-13-93			

DEMCO 38-297